The Carolinas

YESTERDAY — TODAY — TOMORROW

Rockingham Roadside
Maud Gatewood, 1992
Acrylic on canvas
60" x 60.25"
Collection of St. John's Museum of Art,
Wilmington, NC
Gift of Mr. and Mrs. Robert Hobbs

YESTERDAY — TODAY — TOMORROW

AN EXPLORATION OF SOCIAL AND ECONOMIC TRENDS, 1924-1999

by MDC, Inc.

George B. Autry
Ferrel Guillory
Authors and Editors

Leah D. Totten
Managing Editor

Adam S. Mitchell
Associate Editor, Researcher

*This work was commissioned by the Trustees of The Duke Endowment
to commemorate the 75th anniversary of James Buchanan Duke's philanthropy in the Carolinas.*

Hog Series CCXX: The Duke Endowment/In Memory of George Autry
Tarleton Blackwell, 1999
Graphite/Prismacolor/Watercolor
40" x 32"
Courtesy of Hodges Taylor Gallery

For more information on this piece, see *Sources: Literature and Art* on page 101.

THE CAROLINAS

Foreword

On December 11, 1924, Mr. James Buchanan Duke signed the Indenture of Trust that established The Duke Endowment — a private foundation to benefit the people of the Carolinas. For many years, Mr. Duke, his brother Benjamin, and their sister Mary had followed the example set by their father, Washington Duke — taking deliberate and caring steps to aid others less fortunate than they. The creation of The Duke Endowment was, in many ways, a logical extension of a long-time pattern of family giving.

We know that Mr. Duke thought about The Endowment for many years prior to its actual creation. As a successful businessman, he saw the economic and social needs of the Carolinas, and he recognized the transforming power of education. As a devout Methodist, he saw the importance of spiritual life. As a caring human being, he saw the plight of the sick, the aged, the orphaned children. His great dream was to put in place a perpetual source of funds to help address all these needs.

Mr. Duke had a long association with Dr. William Preston Few, president of Trinity College in Durham. Over the years, Dr. Few outlined his own dream — a private university of national stature and leadership, located in the South. Enthralled by Dr. Few's vision, and encouraged by his brother Ben, James B. Duke made it possible for Trinity College to become Duke University — truly a superb demonstration that dreams can come true. It is remarkable that, after 75 years, the foundation still operates as Mr. Duke intended, still addresses the problems and needs he saw, and still cares deeply about the people of the two Carolinas.

As we discussed the 75th anniversary and how to observe it, our thoughts turned, naturally, to all that has been accomplished since 1924. We quickly realized that those achievements belong to our beneficiaries and to the people of the two states. This progress, these accomplishments, these improvements are what we celebrate. This book flowed from that impulse — to look back, but also to look ahead; to see the past and to learn from it what the future may bring. We wanted the book to be informative, but we also wanted it to be beautiful. This was no easy task, and we are immensely grateful to MDC, Inc., and especially to the late George Autry, for their work. George's understanding of our vision and his enthusiasm for the project helped bring this book to life, and the Trustees fondly dedicate it in his memory.

As we look back on three-quarters of a century and we look forward to a new millennium, our heartfelt hope is that this book — our gift to the people of the Carolinas — will be a useful companion in the journey to the future.

— **Mary D.B.T. Semans**
Chairman, The Duke Endowment

Trustees of The Duke Endowment 1999

Mary D.B.T. Semans, *Chairman*

Hugh M. Chapman, *Vice Chairman*

Louis C. Stephens, Jr., *Vice Chairman and 75th Anniversary Chairman*

William G. Anlyan, M.D.

John Hope Franklin, Ph.D.

Constance F. Gray

Richard H. Jenrette

Mary D.T. Jones

Thomas S. Kenan III

Juanita M. Kreps, Ph.D.

Thomas A. Langford, Ph.D.

John G. Medlin, Jr.

Russell M. Robinson II

Minor M. Shaw

Neil Williams

William B. McGuire, *Emeritus*

Charles F. Myers, Jr., *Emeritus*

Dedication

The trustees and staff of The Duke Endowment dedicate this book, with great affection and respect, to the memory of

George B. Autry

His vision shaped this work, his intellect gave it substance, his humanity gave it life.

The Duke Endowment is a private foundation established in 1924 by North Carolina industrialist and philanthropist James B. Duke. The Endowment serves the people of North Carolina and South Carolina by supporting selected programs of higher education, health care, children's welfare, and spiritual life

The Duke Endowment
100 North Tryon Street, Suite 3500
Charlotte, NC 28202-4012
Telephone: (704) 376-0291
Fax: (704) 376-9336
www.dukeendowment.org

MDC Inc. is a private, nonprofit research group that works to expand the economy, develop the workforce, and increase prosperity in communities across the country, with a special focus on the South.

MDC Inc.
P.O. Box 17268
Chapel Hill, NC 27516-7268
Telephone: (919) 968-4531
Fax: (919) 929-8557
www.mdcinc.org

Copyright © 1999 MDC Inc.
Library of Congress Catalog Card Number: 99-047147

Acknowledgments

For us at MDC, publication of this volume represents a bittersweet moment. Our colleague — and friend — George Autry died suddenly only six weeks before completion of the manuscript. As president of MDC, he had been delighted that The Duke Endowment asked us to produce this work. And doing the work — researching, writing, conversing with experts, collecting art and poetry — had stirred in him a sense of challenge, and of fun.

Many of the words that you will read in the chapters that follow were written by George — and his spirit flows from beginning to end. As we moved toward completion, George's wife Bess provided us with insights from her experience as a counselor. Ret Autry Boney had assisted her father in selecting art, and she guided us in completing that task. David Dodson, who was elected by MDC's Board of Directors to succeed George as president, not only gave us his advice on the content but also, importantly, signaled his confidence in our efforts.

Nova Henderson, George's long-time executive assistant, rose to the occasion and increased her already considerable attention to detail, keeping us functioning smoothly. Dr. C.E. Bishop, who became MDC's chief economist after retiring from running major universities, stepped in to check our facts and analysis and to give us his considerable wisdom.

Two members of MDC's staff worked with special diligence, tenacity, and tactfulness in bringing this project to fruition. Leah Totten, the managing editor, kept us on schedule and calmed our nerves. She served as an effective liaison with The Endowment, the graphic designers, and Duke University Press. Adam Mitchell, a recent Duke University graduate who was our associate editor, performed prodigious research, gathering data as well as literature. As the project was ending, he left MDC to join Teach for America, and some California young people along the San Francisco Bay will be fortunate to have him at the head of their classroom.

We gratefully acknowledge the backing of the Board of Directors of MDC, Inc. Our chairman, William Winter, the former governor of Mississippi, and our vice chairman, Juanita Kreps, the former U.S. Secretary of Commerce, offered, as usual, important insights and guidance.

We gratefully acknowledge, too, the backing of the Board of Trustees of The Duke Endowment.

Elizabeth Locke, The Endowment's president, regularly delivered us a dose of her enthusiasm for this project, and her sensitive critiques improved our drafts. Several members of The Endowment's staff provided us important assistance in both process and substance: David Roberson, Joseph Mann, Val Rosenquist, Rhett Mabry.

Fred Chappell, poet laureate of North Carolina, responded generously to our requests for assistance in selecting readings. So, too, did novelists Doris Betts and Reynolds Price. Their work appears herein, but their contributions went beyond what they wrote.

Dot Hodges served as our curator for paintings and photographs. Her efforts, as well as those of Christie Taylor and the staff at Hodges Taylor Gallery, filled the volume with grace notes. Peggy Rabb, Meghan Lubker, and their associates at Southern Media Design and Production, Inc. developed a splendid presentation of this work.

From time to time, we met and drew on the knowledge and experience of thoughtful people who care deeply about the people of the Carolinas. We held consultations, sometimes more than once, with Robert Durden, the Duke historian who has written fine books on The Endowment and the Duke family; George Brown Tindall, the UNC historian who has written several important volumes on the South; Jackson W. Carroll, director of the Ormond Center at the Duke Divinity School; Michael C. Blackwell, president of Baptist Children's Homes of North Carolina; Michael Safley, president of The Methodist Homes for Children of North Carolina; Kevin FitzGerald, director of the North Carolina Division of Social Services; Charles C. Harris, chief of the state Children's Services Section; and James Bernstein, North Carolina's director of rural health. Dennis Lawson at Duke Energy Archives and Janice Palmer at Duke University Medical Center Cultural Services provided valuable assistance with visual art elements of this book.

We deeply appreciate the willingness of Bill Friday, Tom Lambeth, David Shi, Bill Grigg, Susan King, Julius Chambers, and Doris Betts to join our roundtable discussion that is excerpted in Chapter IV.

The MDC project team also warmly recognizes three people who gave us support by tolerating our long hours, understanding our distraction, and striving to keep our lives balanced. We give them a deep bow: Adam Mitchell to Holly Taylor; Leah Totten to Louis Cook, and I to Kat Guillory.

And we offer this report as a contribution to the well-being of the people of the Carolinas, whom George Autry understood so well and to whose advancement he had a lifelong commitment.

— **Ferrel Guillory**

Table of Contents

Preface 1

Chapter I — The Not-So-Roaring '20s 3

Chapter II — The Philanthropic Vision 15

Chapter III — The State of the Carolinas 25

Chapter IV — The Carolinas Tomorrow 69

Roundtable Participants 93

Literary Contributors 95

Visual Arts Contributors 97

Sources: Data and Analysis 99

Sources: Literature and Art 101

THE CAROLINAS

Preface

James Buchanan Duke knew something about being poor; he knew something about being an orphan, and even about being in a minority. He was shaped in childhood by the Civil War to which his widowed father, Washington Duke, objected and into which he was bitterly drafted away from his four young children. It was a war against which Washington Duke made a statement of final rebellion when he joined the Republican Party in 1867, as soon as that party appeared in North Carolina and the rest of the South.

James B. Duke and his siblings were twice unusual. They were raised on a Durham County tobacco farm, the half-orphan children of a single father, in a time when widows headed many families and farms. Their father was also a political outcast: the majority of those women and the decimated corps of white fathers who survived the war were hostile to Republican "scalawags" well into the 20th century.

So James B. Duke knew the barriers and opportunities facing those who grew up in rural North Carolina. He believed that in these rural areas were "the bone and sinew" of society; but he also knew that there was an indigenous, stubborn rural parochialism that could smother progress.

Duke was a business genius. He was also his state's first, best modernizer at the beginning of a half-century struggle between progressives and traditionalists. He applied that spirit of modernization to the rural Carolinas he revered in both his hydroelectric industry and the highly focused philanthropy fueled by that industry.

Mr. Duke completed the legal indenture that established The Duke Endowment in 1924. The focus of this work is what the Carolinas have accomplished since that time — both through The Endowment's investments and otherwise — and what remains to be achieved. The first two chapters set the context of this analysis and the indenture's time and place: the landscape that was the object of Mr. Duke's beneficence in Chapter I and his strategy for improving, even transforming, that landscape in Chapter II. Chapter III describes the state of the Carolinas today in contrast to their state 75 years ago and analyzes broad economic and social trends of the past and present with an eye toward what they may tell us about the future.

Chapter IV is a discussion among distinguished Carolinians about these trends and how Mr. Duke might have confronted them if he were with us and about how the panelists themselves would address the trauma and opportunities that the trends suggest.

The panel focuses partly on the role of foundations, which — more than any other institution in society — are positioned to promote and foster innovation in improving the economic, social, and physical health of individuals, families, and communities.

Mostly Native
Percent of residents foreign-born, 1920

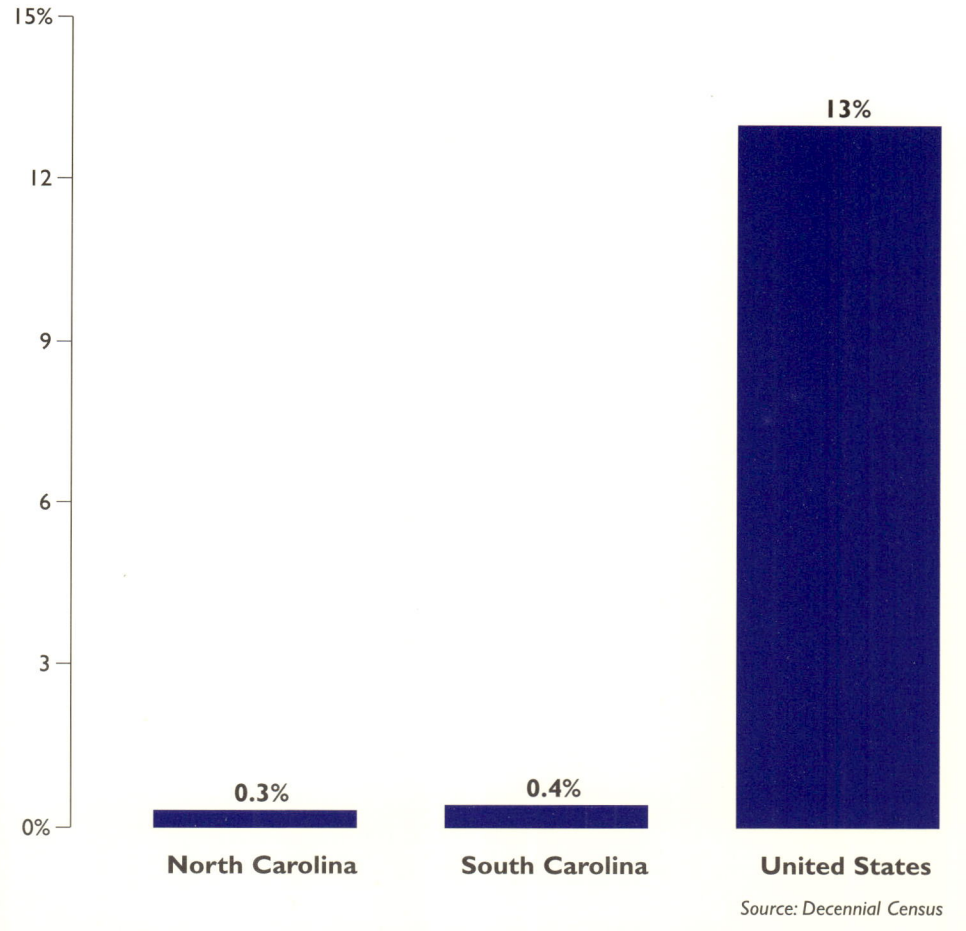

North Carolina	0.3%
South Carolina	0.4%
United States	13%

Source: Decennial Census

overall population, South Carolina had a larger population of blacks — 100,000 more — than did North Carolina. Blacks represented about 30 percent of the North Carolina population and more than 50 percent of the South Carolina population.

The fact that South Carolina had more blacks than whites in the years from 1820 to 1920 helps explain the greater intensity of its racial rigidity. Looking back over the first half of the century, political scientist V.O. Key, Jr. observed:

> South Carolina's preoccupation with the Negro stifles political conflict. Over offices, there is conflict aplenty, but the race issue muffles conflict over issues latent in the economy of South Carolina. Mill worker and plantation owner alike want to keep the Negro in his place.

Still a rural place

Even as an economic revival was sweeping the nation, the South remained largely isolated. And in the Carolinas, an intense dual isolation defined the culture. Not only were most of the people rural, but they lived great distances from one another — isolated from the American mainstream, isolated even from each other. There was, wrote North Carolina sociologist Samuel Huntington Hobbs, an "excessive individualism"

> *And in the Carolinas, an intense dual isolation defined the culture. Not only were most of the people rural, but they lived great distances from one another — isolated from the American mainstream, isolated even from each other.*

and an "excessive rural mindedness."

Individualism and isolation combined to produce a scattering of small churches across the Carolina landscape. Congregations struggled to sustain rickety structures, and ministers were stretched trying to serve these fledgling communities. Hobbs described the North Carolina countryside as "over-churched," with churches outnumbering schoolhouses in many places.

Among the then-48 states, North Carolina and South Carolina ranked in the top five in the percentage of total population living on farms — 60 percent of the two states, compared to the national average of 30 percent.

In both states, small-scale farming was the norm. North Carolina was the state with the fewest cultivated acres per farm dweller — 5.5 acres per person. South Carolina ranked next with 5.7 acres per farm dweller. "We come nearer approaching the European conditions of hand and knee farming than any other state," Hobbs wrote of North Carolina.

In addition, farm tenancy was pervasive. In North Carolina, more than four out of 10 farms were operated by tenants. In South Carolina, half of the farms operated by whites were tenant farms as were 80 percent of the farms operated by blacks.

South Carolina historian G. Croft Williams observed that widespread tenancy had both economic and civic consequences, "for it impoverishes the land" and prevents a large segment of the population from advancing in education and economic well-being.

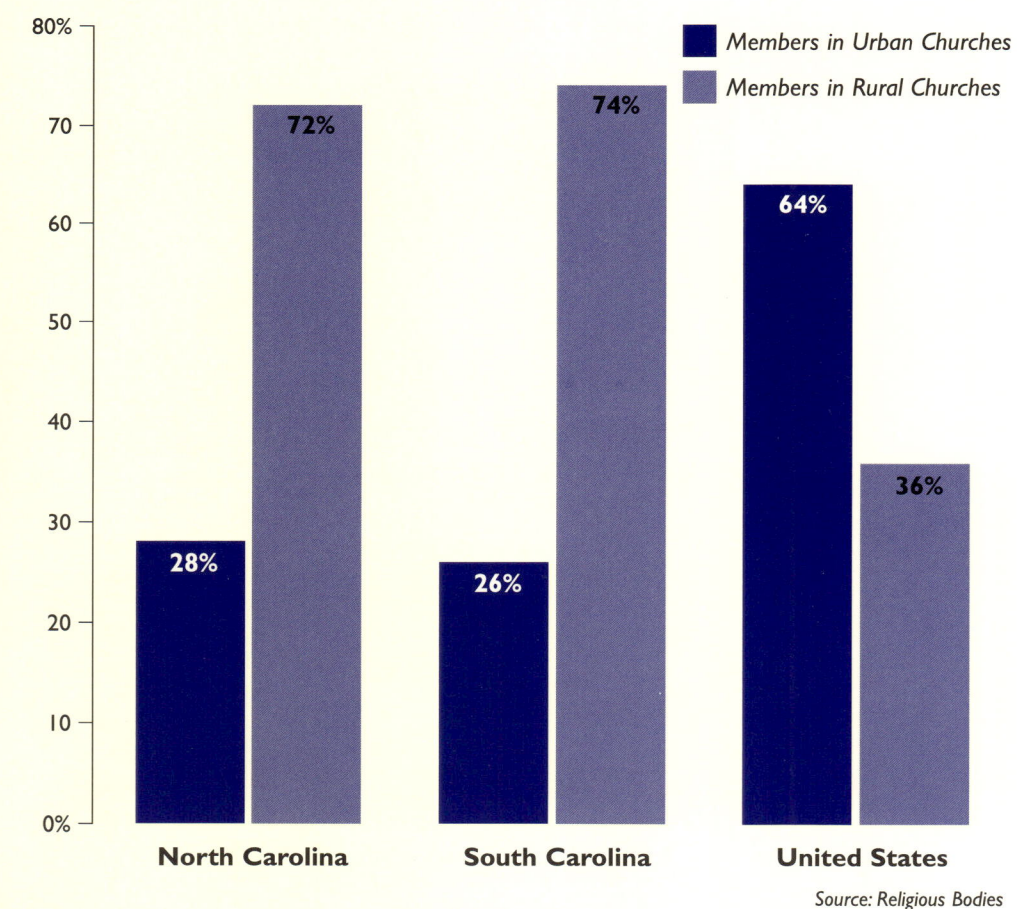

Urban vs. Rural Church Membership, 1926

Source: Religious Bodies

"Sharecropper's Homes"

An excerpt from *The Economic and Social Conditions of Negroes as Tenants and Farm Laborers in South Carolina*, by Walter M. Buchanan

Two Red Shacks
by Beverly Buchanan
25" x 38"
Oil Pastel on Paper
1996

Near the home of each land owner is a group of houses in which croppers live. In one group is about eight small houses not far from the barnyard. These houses are bleak, bare, uninviting and not favored by shade trees. In each yard there are a few beautiful flowers. They have no cultivated land about the house and hence no cotton growing in the yard. The houses generally have two rooms, a front and a rear one. The front room serves as a living-room, dining-room and kitchen. If the houses are painted at all, it is a cheap red paint and all are the same color. The tendency is to have the houses as uniform as possible in every respect except size. The size varies according to the size of the family. On the whole, the houses for croppers are smaller than those of the renter. By the time a man becomes a renter he is older, has been married longer and has a larger family and the necessity for a larger house exists.

The construction of these houses are void of beauty in design and in workmanship. The lumber is crude, rough and unplaned and in every respect without skill and workmanship…

An effort is made to keep the wind out of the house by the use of papers. Newspapers, magazines and wrapping papers, which they have gotten from the stores for the purpose are plastered over the walls of the house and ceiling…

Cropper houses situated at the conjunction of the field and forest are better situated than those near the barnyard. They have more shade and, of course, trees in the yard. The houses are at a distance from each other. This makes the raising of chickens possible without being a likely cause of unfriendly feeling.

…In following a mail route that passes through the center of the plantation … one is led by the stately dwelling of one of the owners to the end of the mail route which ends some distance beyond the dwelling. Here you will find a group of cropper houses about six or more in number standing out in the open cotton field. These are without shade and without yard. Literally cotton grows up to the very door and against the house… The stables were further down at the edge of the woodlot. The mules had the choice location.

Copyright © 1929 by Walter M. Buchanan
Reprinted with permission by Beverly Buchanan

To make matters worse, along came the boll weevil. Both states were cotton country: cotton and tobacco in North Carolina; cotton and corn to the south. Historian George Tindall wrote:

> The worst year was 1921, when the weevil damaged more than 30 percent of the crop and completely wiped out the long-staple Sea Island cotton of South Carolina. [The insect's] invincibility was celebrated in the interminable stanzas of a folk song. The farmer 'buried him in the hot sand... I'll stand it like a man... lef' him on de ice... mighty cool and nice; fed him on paris green... best I ever seen.' 'It is my home,' was his refrain, 'it's jes my home.'

Urbanization and industrialization

Amid excessive ruralness, there were growing towns in the Carolinas. In the 1920 Census, Winston-Salem led the list of North Carolina cities with a population of 48,400, about 2,000 more than Charlotte. Wilmington was third, with 33,370, about 9,000 people more than Raleigh. In South Carolina, Charleston was the most populous city with 68,000 people, 30,000 more than Columbia. Though the Carolinas' towns didn't match the cities of the North in terms of size, they adapted to technological and cultural change. For instance, Charlotte's WBT, the Carolinas' first radio station, went on the air in 1921, only a year after KDKA in Pittsburgh inaugurated commercial broadcasting in the United States.

During and after World War I, more and more Carolinians began working by the clock inside rather than by the sun outside. In the '20s, the Carolinas were, simultaneously, predominantly rural and increasingly industrial. In a poor but rather stable society, change elbowed its way in.

Economically, North Carolina had a broader industrial base while South Carolina developed an economy centered around large textile mills. By the mid-'20s, North Carolina had become the South's leading manufacturing state — with tobacco, textiles, and furniture, the industries that would dominate during the 20th century, leading the way.

Several factors contributed to the Carolinas'

> *During and after World War I, more and more Carolinians began working by the clock inside rather than by the sun outside. In the '20s, the Carolinas were, simultaneously, predominantly rural and increasingly industrial. In a poor but rather stable society, change elbowed its way in.*

The Republic Cotton Mills of Great Falls, SC, in 1915.

Photo courtesy of Duke Power Archives

attraction as a locale for these types of manufacturing: abundant raw materials, cheap labor, low cost of living, and water power. Indeed, the harnessing of water power by Mr. Duke's utility and others supplied the electricity that turned the spindles and otherwise fueled an enormous shift in the economy. Cash summarized the progression this way:

> Under the touch of Buck Duke's millions, hydroelectric power sprang into being, and by 1910 the energy of a million horses was pulsing into the wires of Dixie. And literally a hundred lesser industries made their appearance. By 1914, apart from the cotton mills, there were at least 15,000 manufacturing establishments of one sort or another in the South; and though most of them were exceedingly small, yet in the aggregate the value of their product far exceeded that of the cotton mills themselves.

And side by side with this went a tremendous growth and multiplication of towns.

Illiteracy and ill health

Illiteracy ran rampant in the Carolinas of the 1920s. Today's South worries about functional illiteracy: the inability to read, write, and figure well enough to function in a technological society and a modern labor market. When The Duke Endowment was founded, measurements of illiteracy went by the classic definition: the inability to read and write, period.

Among North Carolinians age 10 and above, 24 percent of blacks and 8 percent of whites were counted as illiterates in 1920. In South Carolina, 29 percent of blacks and 6 percent of whites could not read and write. While no figures were available at that time, Hobbs suggested that the people suffering from "near-illiteracy" outnumbered those in sheer illiteracy. Farm tenancy and rural isolation contributed to high levels of both illiteracy and near-illiteracy; tenancy required no education for adults, and to export children off the farm to school was often too expensive in terms of both money and lost labor.

The 20th century opened with something of an education reform movement sweeping across the South, and in the 1920s state and local governments assumed responsibility for school programs that had been launched by national foundations. South Carolina led eight Southern states that exceeded the national rate of increase in cost per pupil. "There was reason for pride in the achievement," wrote Tindall, "but one educational leader warned that the South was 'in grave danger of ballyhooing itself into further backwardness.'"

In the Carolinas, school attendance dropped off markedly at age 15. Nearly 80 percent of 14- to 15-year-olds were in school in 1920, but only 50 percent of 16- to 17-year-olds.

Disease was as common as illiteracy. By the mid-1920s, South Carolina had more than 80 deaths per 100,000 people from tuberculosis and 40 per 100,000 from pellagra. The state had 17,000 cases of malaria in 1927. Not only was infant mortality high, so was maternal mortality — more than eight mothers died for every 1,000 births in North Carolina in 1925.

An early report from The Duke Endowment illustrates the paucity of hospitals available to Carolinians in 1925:

> For the country as a whole there is one general hospital bed for every 291 people; ...for North Carolina there is one general hospital bed for every 517 people.... North Carolina is the fortieth State in the Union in the proportion of population to hospital beds; ...[f]or South Carolina there is one general hospital bed for every 797 people.... South Carolina is the forty-eighth State

> **Forty-four of North Carolina's 100 counties had no general hospitals at all while 21 of South Carolina's 46 counties were similarly bereft of hospital facilities.**

in the Union in the proportion of population to hospital beds.

Forty-four of North Carolina's 100 counties had no general hospitals at all while 21 of South Carolina's 46 counties were similarly bereft of hospital facilities. Of North Carolina's 102 general hospitals (which had bed space for 3,753 white patients and 949 black patients), 72 were private and 30 were public. South Carolina in 1926 had 46 general hospitals with bed space for 1,598 white patients and 714 black patients; 28 of those 46 hospitals were private.

Photo courtesy of Duke Power Archives

An electric range float in Greenville, SC, in 1927

Reform — and reaction

The 18th Amendment, approved in 1919, went into effect as 1920 dawned in the United States. Josephus Daniels, the Raleigh newspaper publisher who served as the Wilson Administration's Secretary of the Navy, welcomed in Prohibition at a church assembly in Washington in January 1920.

From then on, as Tindall wrote, the decade featured two conflicting images of the South: "the benighted South and the progressive New South." And in that era, progressivism contained, simultaneously, a good-government strain and a moral-righteousness strain. It was during the 1920s that North Carolina won its reputation as the "Wisconsin of the South," a reference to the preeminent good-government state of the nation.

But in addition to education and health initiatives, as well as road-building, the Carolinas also indulged in movements to resist the rush into modernity. If it was a time of modest reform, it was also a time, as Cash wrote, of "fears and hates."

Southerners in Congress had voted for Prohibition more heavily than representatives of other states. And more than a few of their constituents promptly made the region infamous for its white lightnin'.

The 1920s also featured a rash of "monkey bills" — efforts in Southern legislatures to prevent the teaching of Darwin's theory of evolution. South Carolina turned aside one such bill in 1921. Four years later, the North Carolina General Assembly considered a bill to prohibit the teaching of evolution in the public colleges and schools of the state, a bill that led then-state Representative Sam J. Ervin, Jr., to deliver the sort of vivid down-home speech for which he became famous in Washington a half-century later. Ervin declared:

> If my friends had been sitting in the Spanish legislature when Columbus undertook, with Queen Isabella's financial assistance, to make his first voyage of discovery to America, they would undoubtedly have proposed legislation to prohibit his sailing for fear he might fall

> *The monkeys in the jungle would undoubtedly be delighted to know that the North Carolina Legislature has absolved them from all responsibility for the conduct of the human race in general and that of the North Carolina Legislature in particular.*
>
> — Sam J. Ervin, Jr.

Photo courtesy of Duke Power Archives

Mule teams at the square on a Saturday morning in Spartanburg, SC, in 1900.

off one of the four corners of the earth. Although I am adamantly opposed to the Poole bill, candor compels me to confess that its passage would produce one happy result. The monkeys in the jungle would undoubtedly be delighted to know that the North Carolina Legislature has absolved them from all responsibility for the conduct of the human race in general and that of the North Carolina Legislature in particular.

In parallel with the surge of antievolution fever, the Ku Klux Klan had a resurgence during the 1920s. At that time, it was an organization composed of whites who worked on the farm and in the mill, of small businessmen, and of politicians. Many of the more prominent businessmen who did not join nevertheless winked. The Klan, wrote Cash, "summed up within itself, with precise completeness and exactness, the whole body of the fears and hates of the time," and he went on to say:

> It was, as is well known, at once anti-Negro, anti-Alien, anti-Red, anti-Catholic, anti-Jew, anti-Darwin, anti-Modern, anti-Liberal, fundamentalist, vastly Moral, militantly Protestant. And, summing up these fears, it brought them into focus with the tradition of the past, and above all with the ancient Southern pattern of high romantic histrionics, violence and mass coercion of the scapegoat and the heretic.

THE NOT-SO-ROARING '20S

So, as the end of the Great War ushered in the beginnings of modern American society, it also set in motion a time of turbulence in the rural, small-town, white-Protestant Carolinas.

For the rest of the United States, the 1920s were the decade of jazz, of the introduction of radio and the proliferation of automobile ownership, of the first stages of the liberation of women, and of the hero-worship of Babe Ruth and Charles Lindbergh. But for the Carolinas, the 1920s were a decade of persistent poverty and ignorance, of a mixture of moralism and progressivism, of a creeping toward urbanism and a fear of what technological change would mean to a culture that had long resisted change.

By the time The Duke Endowment went into action, conflicting economic and social currents had come together in the Carolinas. Reform vied with reaction. The city lured people away from the countryside. Economic growth lifted hopes, but persistent poverty left many behind in hopelessness. In the midst of these paradoxes, Mr. Duke's Endowment went to work on the tasks of transforming a hidebound society and helping people lift themselves to a higher quality of life in a region about which he cared deeply.

Chapter II
The Philanthropic Vision

Photo courtesy of The Duke Endowment

"*For many years I have been engaged in the development of water powers in certain sections of the States of North and South Carolina. In my study of the subject I have observed how such utilization of a natural resource, which otherwise would run in waste to the sea and not remain and increase as a forest, both gives impetus to industrial life and provides a safe and enduring investment for capital. My ambition is that the revenues of such developments shall administer to the social welfare, as the operation of such developments is administering to the economic welfare, of the communities which they serve.*"

— **James B. Duke in the Indenture and Deed of Trust establishing The Duke Endowment, December 11, 1924.**

"As I have thought of your plan, it grows in my mind. I think it is really a sounder idea than that around which any other large benevolence in this country with which I am familiar has been built."

— **William Preston Few, the first president of Duke University, in a letter to Mr. Duke in 1919.**

James B. Duke (right) with his brother Benjamin in Atlantic City, 1924.

Photo courtesy of Duke University Archives

James Buchanan "Buck" Duke once noted — as have many since — that making his money had been easier than finding a way to give it away wisely. But he did find a way. That unique way reinvested the profits generated from the Carolinas' natural resources in the two states' human resources.

John D. Rockefeller preceded Duke as one of the leading industrialists and philanthropists of his day by harnessing the economic potential of a different natural resource: oil. Unlike Duke, however, he, Carnegie, and others spread their giving across the country and even around the world. Rockefeller, for example, rarely directed philanthropic dollars to the communities where oil was pumped or refined.

Mr. Duke, by contrast, saw Duke Power Company and The Duke Endowment as institutions with complementary missions: the first enabling the industrial and economic development of the North Carolina and South Carolina Piedmont; the second supporting the development

> *Mr. Duke, by contrast, saw the Duke Power Company and The Duke Endowment as institutions with complementary missions: the first enabling the industrial and economic development of the North Carolina and South Carolina Piedmont; the second supporting the development of the Carolinas' people along "physical, mental, and spiritual lines."*

of the Carolinas' people along "physical, mental, and spiritual lines." He invested deeply in this geographic area defined by his heritage and business interests, explaining in his indenture that he "might have extended this aid to other charitable objects and to other sections, but my opinion is that so doing would be productive of less good by reason of attempting too much." In addition to this unique conceptual framework, there was also a variety of functional originality in The Endowment — from the leverage and focus of the benefaction to its detailed instructions for governance.

In the 1880s, Andrew Carnegie said, "Neither the individual nor the race is improved by almsgiving." Carnegie acted on his notion that charity by itself only perpetuates what it seeks to ameliorate. He pioneered philanthropy "that provides the ladders upon which the aspiring can rise… to assist but rarely or never to do all." His would be a philanthropy that encouraged improvement, collaboration, and creative problem-solving.

> *In a time when most philanthropists' giving was in reaction to requests or the advice of "professionals," Mr. Duke's indenture reflects the benefactor and is a product of his personal experiences and convictions. It is humanitarian and egalitarian, with the repeated injunction that The Endowment serve "both white and colored" in a society that was then crippled by Jim Crow.*

This expansive definition of philanthropy was the one Mr. Duke introduced to the South by polishing, focusing, and formalizing his family's strong legacy of giving. For years before The Duke Endowment was established, Washington Duke and his children gave to the Methodist Church, a liberal arts college then known as Trinity, the Oxford Orphan Asylum, and other charities. In addition, the Duke family received and honored countless requests for money from relatives and even poor strangers. By creating The Duke Endowment in 1924, Mr. Duke set in motion a trust that would systematize his giving and would target several of the Carolinas' most pressing social problems comprehensively and in perpetuity.

In a time when most philanthropists' giving was in reaction to requests or the advice of "professionals," Mr. Duke's indenture reflects the benefactor and is a product of his personal experiences and convictions. It is humanitarian and egalitarian, with the repeated injunction that The Endowment serve "both white and colored"

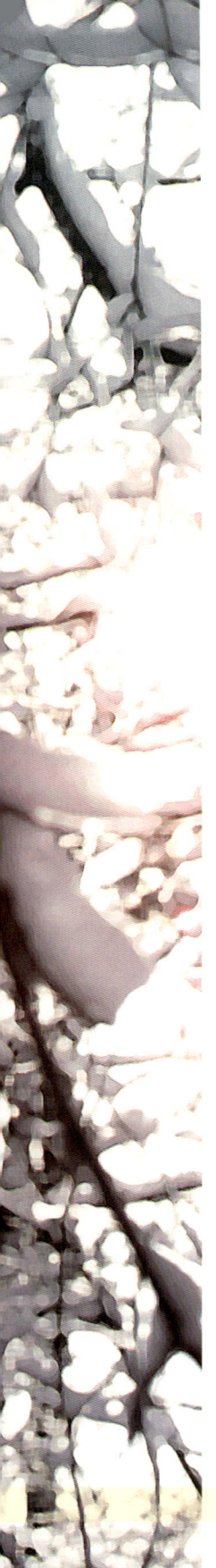

"The Recovery of Human Compassion"

An excerpt from *Sermons from the Black Pulpit* by Samuel Proctor

Some years ago when I was doing college work in the South, I went to eastern Carolina to Nash County to give a speech at a 4-H Club conference. In those days everything was segregated, and this was a black 4-H Club conference. In those days college heads routinely attended such conferences because we felt that rural young people benefitted from such visits.

I listened carefully to the young man who spoke before I was to speak, and I was moved. He was very bright.

When he turned around, I shook his hand to congratulate him, and he blushed bashfully. But when he opened his eyes, I saw that one eye was severely astigmatized. We call it "crossed"; his eye was severely "crossed."

One eye sank right down in the corner, and it struck me forcefully. I thought to myself, *You mean that boy has a problem like that?* And my mind kept turning, and I forgot all about my little remarks.

I kept on saying, *Sam, here you are healthy and prosperous. You drove out here in a brand new car. You've got credit cards spilling out of your wallet. You're loaded down with Smithfield ham and orange juice, grits and oatmeal! Your eyes are perfect. Why don't you do something for that boy?* And I tried to say to myself, *I can't be bothered.* I tried to sneak past on the other side of the Jericho road; *I'm too busy for that detail. Somebody else will catch him.*

As I was riding back with our school public relations man, he said to me, "Your mind is blank, Sam.

in a society that was then crippled by Jim Crow. There are also more subtle reflections of Mr. Duke in the indenture. For example, he was fascinated by the construction and problem-solving challenges presented by the electric power business. He was equally challenged by the complexity of founding a philanthropy that formed deep, lasting relationships with core beneficiaries who would gain sophistication from sustained support.

Mr. Duke's indenture laid out four areas of concern: higher education, health care, and children's care in North Carolina and South Carolina, and the rural Methodist Church in a predominantly rural North Carolina. This was a philanthropy able to take the long-term view and work with a limited number of partner institutions in a variety of ways over an extended period of time. The indenture also made it clear that The Endowment was not to be a crutch on which beneficiaries could lean — it was to leverage and enable their own efforts, not supplant them. For example, the community and congregation had to raise as much or more money themselves in order to receive Endowment support.

You're not talking to me." And I said, "Yeah, yeah, yeah, that's right." But God had just put it on me: "Sam, I'm not going to let you go. You saw that little country boy with those crossed eyes. You don't have anybody in your family with crossed eyes. What are you going to do?" I could hardly sleep that night.

Later I told the public-relations staff person that I wanted him to ride back over there and I wanted to find that boy. "What boy?" "The little boy with the crossed eyes." "Oh, come on, Sam, the boy's eyes have been crossed all of his life." I said, "No, I can't drop it like that, because I'm burdened with it." You keep on getting burdened if you try to let Christ lead your life; but the burden is light and his yoke is an easy yoke.

We went out there and we found him. (I had asked a county agricultural agent to get his name and address and the directions to his home.) We took one road and another road and another road, and deep into Nash County we found the little house. There we found all of the poverty and isolation that were so typical of the rural south at that time. When we spoke to his mother about helping him

continued...

The Miracle of the Loaves and Fishes
Gerald Steinmeyer
Fresco
Life size, totaling 64 square feet
Courtesy of the congregation, Germanton United Methodist Church
(See *Sources: Literature and Art* on page 101 for more information.)

Able-minded, able-bodied

Mr. Duke's focus on the power of higher education was both novel and prescient for his time. He claimed in the indenture that "education, when conducted along sane and practical, as opposed to dogmatic and theoretical, lines, is, next to religion, the greatest civilizing influence." The power of Mr. Duke's idea — that education should neither be locked in an ivory tower nor restricted to denominational doctrine, but instead should be useful and applied for the benefit of humanity —

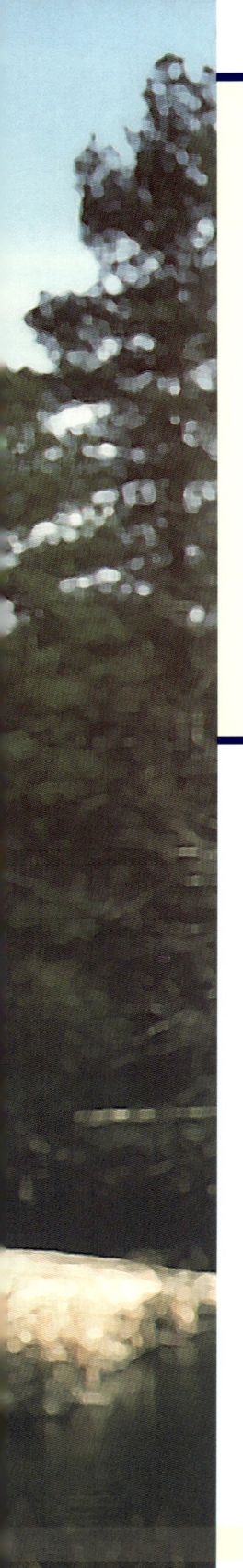

get surgery for his eye, she said, "The Lord made him like that; leave him like that." He said, "Will it hurt, Dr. Proctor?" I said, "If they do it, it's not going to hurt." "Who's going to do it?" "I don't know yet, but I know one thing; big as this world is and the way I'm burdened with this, if there's anybody around here who knows how to straighten out crossed eyes, he's my man and I'll find him." His mother finally gave a slow, qualified agreement.

When we came back to Greensboro, we didn't know what to do. I was reading a book on ethics by Waldo Beach. I knew Waldo Beach; he was a Duke University ethics professor. I went to see him.

"Brother Beach," I said, "you must know somebody in Durham who's big enough, an ophthalmologist with enough compassion, to straighten out one little black boy's crossed eyes." He said, "Sam, I go to a church where there's a father and his two sons who run an eye clinic in Durham. And they do that operation all the time. They are Christian folk. And if this thing is burdening you the way it is, then I'm going to burden them with it, too."

The next day the phone rang. Waldo Beach said to me, "Sam, the doctor and his dad and his brother said they'll do it if I get the boy to them." Compassion. I rushed back over to Nash County.

Now I know that the world still has its problems. I couldn't feed every hungry child in India. I couldn't solve the problems of women's rights. I couldn't solve the civil rights problem. But God will take you as God took me, and focus you on something, and then test you and see what you're going to do with it.

I went back over to Nash County and told the boy and his mother the good news. His mama

has been as important as the power of his money.

At Duke University, which receives the largest share of The Endowment's funding, Mr. Duke's money enabled the realization of his vision. Trinity College, a small Methodist liberal arts college, became the central core of first a regional and then national university. Now Duke University serves the world: Duke scholars apply Duke research in the sciences and humanities to problems of law, health, business, the environment, and education around the world. And what began as a modest hospital and the Carolinas' first four-year medical school has developed into a medical center that serves both its local region and heads of state, as well as ordinary folk, from abroad.

While The Endowment's investment in its three other educational beneficiaries — Davidson College, Furman University, and Johnson C. Smith University — has been less, its ongoing support and guidance have steadily strengthened the institutions and their capacity to serve humanity.

Mr. Duke was also convinced that a critical challenge facing the Carolinas in the 1920s was improving health care in a region overwhelmed started crying and praying. She said, "We'll have him there."

Now to make a long story short, his eyes were straightened out. Later on, he asked if I would write a reference for him to go to Livingstone College, and he made one of the finest records they ever had there. Some time after that, when I was at the University of Wisconsin, he said, "I'd like to come up there and get my Master of Business Administration degree." I got him in there, and he ripped right through that MBA. He ended up in Pittsburgh working for the Gulf Oil Company.

A little while ago, I was sitting in my office and he walked in and said, "I'm a product manager for Johnson and Johnson across the street." He said to me just before leaving, "Dr. Proctor, I want to ask you something for my own benefit. What made you take an interest in me?"

I said, "Well, I went to school a long time studying about Jesus, and I promised him over and over that I would serve him until I died. You just gave me one of the best opportunities to do just that and I seized upon it."

He asked further, "What made Dr. Beach want to do it? What made those white ophthalmologists in Durham give me a free operation like that?" "Because they're Christian folk, too. They love the Lord, too." And if you get enough folk like that, loving Jesus like that, reaching across race and clan, showing compassion, one day the kingdoms of this world *will indeed* become the kingdom of our God and of his Christ.

Sermons from the Black Pulpit
by Samuel D. Proctor and William D. Watley
Copyright © 1984 by Judson Press, Valley Forge, PA
Reprinted with permission of Judson Press

---

by curable diseases. Support for medical research, technology, and education had long been a mainstay of Rockefeller's philanthropy, whose Sanitary Commission began eradication of the hookworm.

Mr. Duke's solution to improving rural health care was to attract more physicians by providing community hospitals with the most modern equipment available and to help pay for the charity care given by such hospitals. The great majority of hospitals in operation were privately owned and therefore closed to many physicians and patients. Fees were prohibitive, especially for the rural poor. Though many at the time argued that ill or injured country folk should travel to the nearest city for care, The Endowment's 10th annual report clearly states Mr. Duke's position: "The rural population is entitled to just as good medical care… as people in large cities." This reflected Mr. Duke's desire to improve the quality of rural life by moving resources in, instead of forcing people to move out. His Endowment's theories and methods were so effective that they later provided the model for the federal government's Hill-Burton Act which put billions of dollars into hospital construction.

THE PHILANTHROPIC VISION

Children and churches

Before he was two years old, James Buchanan Duke was himself half-orphaned by his mother's death. He was effectively parentless for the years his father was serving in the Civil War. Reflecting his own understanding of the challenges facing orphans and wanting to expand on the Duke family's long-standing relationship with the Oxford Orphan Asylum, Mr. Duke included in The Endowment's indenture the care of "white or colored whole or half orphans" in institutions in the Carolinas. In 1926 the Endowment contributed $10 per orphan to 35 institutions serving 4,677 young people.

But as was the case with all its beneficiaries, orphanages got critical professional and technical assistance from The Endowment. The Endowment helped institutions develop a uniform system of record keeping, established a clearinghouse of best practices in the operation of child-care institutions, and started the process of creating a system of minimum standards for the care of children in group homes. In addition, all of The Endowment's beneficiaries,

Downtown Charlotte, NC, in 1924.

Photo courtesy of Duke Power Archives

22

THE CAROLINAS

including children's homes, were able to continue operating through the Depression as many of their counterparts had to shut their doors.

In another bow to his own heritage and to his family's philanthropic legacy, Mr. Duke's Endowment made provisions for the rural Methodist Church of North Carolina. His father credited the Church and its circuit-riding preachers as one of the largest influences in his life, and Washington Duke supported it financially in accordance. This same belief was passed down to his children: Buck Duke once said: "If I amount to anything in this world, I owe it to my daddy and the Methodist Church."

The Endowment was charged with helping to build and maintain rural churches in North Carolina, helping support retired pastors and their survivors, and assisting with the churches' operational costs. But The Endowment never supplied more than half those costs and always pushed congregations to build a lasting, architecturally sound structure with ample facilities for Sunday School. The Endowment also commissioned architectural models for small rural churches, an important initiative that raised the standard of church facilities and buildings. By enabling the building, operation, or renovation of churches in many small and isolated communities, The Endowment kept whole and vital the social and religious life of many rural communities.

While the operational support for orphanages and rural churches, as well as the money provided to "worn-out preachers," is a limited beneficence to causes close to Mr. Duke's heart, they suggested that systems were needed to take care of disrupted families and the elderly. As a precursor to Social Security and other government support programs, The Endowment's work with those unable to help themselves showed that focused resources and energy (and not random charity) were the foundations of a healthy society.

A perpetual trust

James B. Duke's philanthropy dug deep into the social problems of two of the poorest states in America at a time when foundations were commonly given generalized mandates with no limits, focus, or structure for addressing problems. The South was mired in poverty and could easily have been a black hole for the meager philanthropic dollars invested in the region. That The Endowment vastly improved, and continues today to improve, the areas it addressed serves as

a philanthropic model. So too is the financial success of The Endowment a model: gifts from Mr. Duke for grant-making valued at just over $90 million in 1925 have produced grants worth $1.388 billion through December 1998 even as The Endowment's assets have continued to grow to well over $2 billion.

The Endowment now plows the same ground in a vastly changed environment. More universities, hospitals, churches, and orphanages are not the needs they were in Mr. Duke's time — partly because of Mr. Duke. But creation of knowledge and the capacity to apply it, access to health care, spiritual reflection amidst cultural bombardment, nurture of children in fragmented families — all these are challenges as fresh and various as they are enduring.

CHAPTER III

The State of the Carolinas

By all economic and most social measures, this is the Golden Age of the Carolinas. The people of the two states are healthier, more prosperous, and better educated than ever. Their great-grandparents in the 1920s could hardly have imagined a society that is so thoroughly integrated into mainstream America and so well positioned to compete in the global economy.

"Everything that was ever possible for civilized man is possible here," Walter Lippmann wrote of the South in the 1920s. Then as now, the South possessed the natural and human resources with which to flourish. But unfortunately, then and for decades thereafter, the South lagged in marshalling and investing in its resources.

By the time Lippmann wrote those words, James Buchanan Duke and The Endowment he created had begun to help erect facilities in the Carolinas necessary for "civilized man" — places

for teaching and learning, for healing, for sheltering the young, and for worshiping. Mr. Duke and the people who have run his philanthropy through the decades have proved that investing in the South's people pays handsomely.

The Carolinas' experience over the past seven decades gives resounding evidence of the potency not only of such philanthropy but also of progressive leadership and public and private investments.

Sometimes, of course, the importance of forward-looking leadership was demonstrated by its opposite, or its absence. From time to time, Carolinians — rank-and-file citizens as well as their leaders — worked harder to maintain racial segregation and the economic status quo than to respond to distress and disease. During the Great Depression, the Carolinas were among the poorest of the American states, worse off than even the poorest state outside the South.

World War II served, in the words of historian Dewey W. Grantham, as a "transforming experience" for the Carolinas as well as for the South. Less than a decade after President Roosevelt's special commission declared the South the nation's "No. 1 economic problem," his administration deliberately used the war mobilization as a means of modernizing the South. Grantham wrote:

---

en route to hamlet was inspired by my trips down Highway 74. On this side of Rockingham and Hamlet, there is a singular, three-story brick wall in a field of kudzu. Perhaps it is what remains of a turn-of-the-century mill. Its arched windows make it resemble an aqueduct with kudzu growing up the side. It's the greatest unintentional piece of public art in the southeast. Hamlet is where John Coltrane was born, hamlet is a small town, and these images are about a journey — sometimes down rural roads, sometimes down my imagination, sometimes in the place I am currently sitting. —**Tom Stanley**

The war encouraged the national economic integration of the South and significantly reduced the economic and social disparities between Southerners and other Americans. It led to an infusion of new capital and industry into the South, quickened the pace of its urbanization, accelerated the restructuring of its agriculture and brought a flood of soldiers to Southern training camps from other regions.

In the aftermath of the war, the federal government made critical long-term educational investments that helped further transform the South. The G.I. Bill enabled military veterans to attend college and thus provided the region with more brainpower to fuel its transformation. The National Science Foundation, among other initiatives, broadened the research capacity of universities and thus served to foster the institutional development of Southern higher education.

Congress passed the Hill-Burton Act in 1946, leading to the realization of one of Mr. Duke's dreams — a hospital in nearly every county. The National Institutes of Health charted a course to help alleviate the health problems of the nation, including the South.

At the end of the war, unfortunately, the South also turned anew to fighting old fights. The white South, in particular, reacted sharply to legal pressure from the federal government and moral pressure from the civil rights movement to dismantle racial segregation laws. And yet, once Jim Crow collapsed, private investment flowed in and economic growth accelerated — leading to increased prosperity for whites along with blacks. At critical moments, leaders emerged

en route to hamlet
Tom Stanley,
1993-99
Acrylic on canvas
13.75" x 13.75" each
Photographs by
Terry Roueche

THE STATE OF THE CAROLINAS

to guide the states through a transition in race relations and to advocate for investments in education, training, and infrastructure that permitted the Carolinas to participate in the Sunbelt surge. Two examples illustrate the point:

In his single term as governor of North Carolina, Terry Sanford, who was later president of Duke University and a U.S. senator, built up his state's community college system, launched a pioneering antipoverty effort through The North Carolina Fund, and convinced the legislature to raise taxes to bolster the public schools. Sanford's contemporary, Ernest F. Hollings, who served a term as South Carolina's governor and then more than 30 years as a U.S. senator, initiated an industrialization campaign, worked to assure the peaceful integration of Clemson University, and subsequently took "hunger tours" around his state to build support for food, housing, and medical programs.

The two major rights movements that swept across America in mid-century have contributed to the transformation of the Carolinas. Our states have witnessed — and been strengthened by — the burgeoning of a strong black middle class and the dynamism of women in education and the economy.

Still, just at the point at which our two states are catching up with the country, they have run smack into the new hurdles arising from demographic shifts, the global economy, and higher citizen expectations. The big-picture trends that are shaping the near-term future of the Carolinas are not reversible, but the Carolinas can give their people the wherewithal to cope and even to flourish.

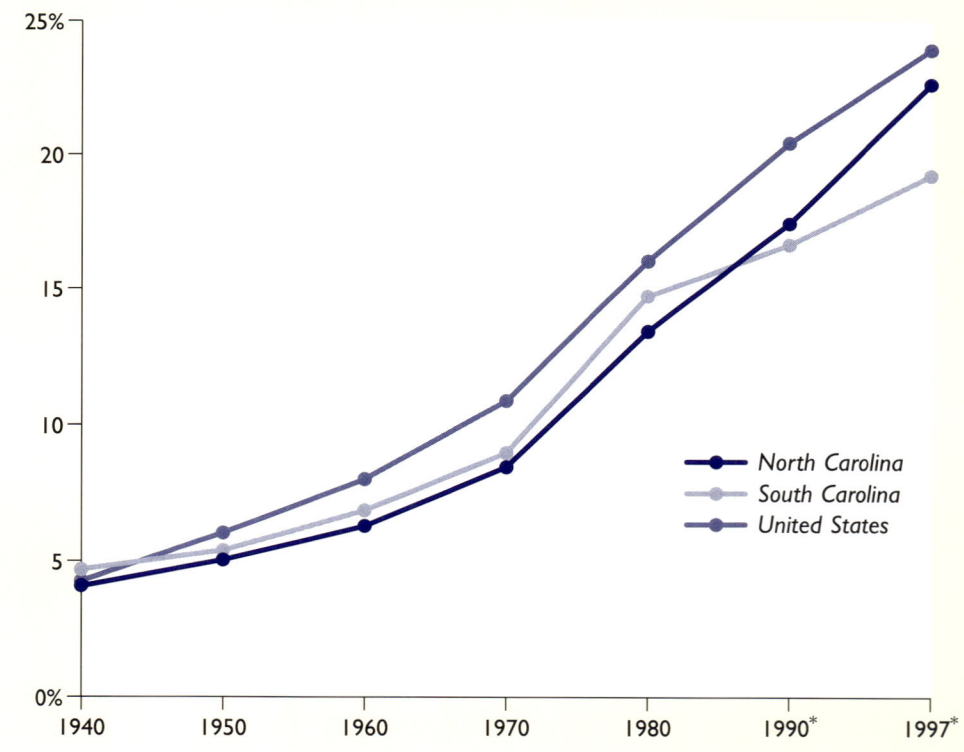

More Brain Power
Percent NC, SC, and U.S. populations 25 years and older with at least four years of college / BA degree

*Data only available by state as BA+
Source: Decennial Census and Current Population Survey

More muscle, more confidence

As they confront the new hurdles, the people of the Carolinas have already proved, to others and to themselves, that they can succeed in a changing economy and society, that they can be the engine and not the caboose:

- Durham, where the Duke family made its cigarettes, has become an international center of medicine and higher education, a linchpin of the flourishing Research Triangle. The Research Triangle Park, developed on the strength of nearby universities (including the one Mr. Duke transformed through his philanthropy), grew into a major center of information technology, biotechnology, and pharmaceuticals.
- In North Carolina's universities, there are more top-20 doctoral programs than in any other state of the South.
- Charlotte, where Mr. Duke planted his power company, has evolved from a town where textile executives went for financing into a national and global banking and commercial center.
- Greenville/Spartanburg transformed itself from a cotton-mill economy into a high-tech automotive center as it became a catch basin for German and other direct foreign investment.
- Charleston, that graceful coastal city, has survived a massive hurricane and military downsizing to reemerge as a thriving center of commerce and culture.
- The Carolinas invented a new model of education based on an economic imperative as they designed community colleges to retool the workforce and to attract new businesses.

Along with boosting public and private investment in universities and hospitals, the Carolinas diversified their economies. Information technologies and improved highways and airports — and, of course, airconditioning — made the Carolinas more attractive for industrial facilities and high-rise office buildings. As a result of diversification, our two states absorbed substantial job-shedding by the textile and tobacco industries over two decades, to the point that their unemployment rates at the end of the 1990s fell well below the nation's. Thus, having leaped over substantial barriers, the Carolinas can face the future with confidence — knowing, as Lippmann said, that everything is possible here.

Rural no longer

The industrial age has been a race toward the city. Carolinians have found themselves pulled — many willingly, some reluctantly — into the race, although the pace was slowed by the profitability of small tobacco farms and by textile mills located in small towns strung along the states' waterways. By the 1990s, it was clear that the "bone and sinew" that Mr. Duke wanted to strengthen in the country was muscling up in the city. The two-mule farm has given way to two-car garages in sprawling suburbs, often built on sites where cotton, corn, and tobacco once grew.

As recently as 1986, in his book *The New Heartland*, John Herbers, a national correspondent for *The New York Times*, held North Carolina up as "the prototype for America's future" in its active invitation to a style of living characterized by low-density growth. Even as the two states have become more cosmopolitan, the Carolinas have avoided the dense urban development that Southerners find so unattractive in the North. Our cities feature many safe, leafy neighborhoods that appeal to longtime residents and recent arrivals alike.

And yet, in creating automobile-dependent suburbanized cities, the people of the Carolinas come to the end of the 20th century faced with an array of new challenges: how to tame sprawl that eats up precious landscape, how to reduce the fouling of air and water, and how to build nurturing communities and a vital civic life in an often-impersonal society. For many Carolinians, a house on a grassy lot with a back deck along a safe cul-de-sac represents the American dream come true. However unintentional, that lifestyle,

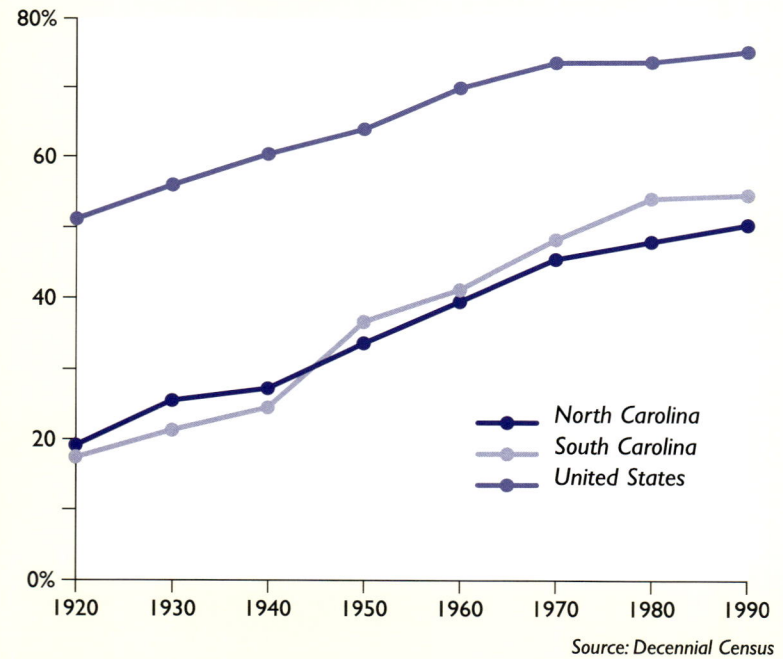

Carolinians Become City Folks
Percent of residents living in urban areas — NC, SC, and U.S., 1920-1990

Source: Decennial Census

A Wilson County Farmer

by James Applewhite

The mercury-vapor yard light on a pole
    comes on automatically at dusk, triggered
it seems by the television's phosphorescent glow in
    the front room, seen incongruously through those
sashes and panes from just after the Civil War.
    The middle-aged farmer standing in shadow of this
unnatural light before his packhouse, still smoking
    a Lucky, just a few in any day now, sees
heads of his wife and daughter-in-law through the
    window, and the grandson's occasional, ball-quick
passage through color, and thinks maybe he has survived
    too long. Life is easier, maybe, with MH-30
to inhibit suckers, the tractor-drawn harvesters,
    where croppers ride close to the ground, breaking
off leaves, clipping them into the reeled chains. But hands
    are undependable, and without his blood kin,
a man couldn't hardly be sure of a harvest crew.
    Some use the migrants, hard-working, ignorant
of the ways of tobacco. With the quotas, the declining
    prices, every day more news about cancer, this man
who learned tobacco from his father, who himself couldn't
    read and write, looks far across at red Antares
over the swamp woods there beyond the highway, not knowing
    what star he is seeing, and feels his station in this
place lit by blue light and T.V. as odd and as lonely.

"A Wilson County Farmer" by James Applewhite
From *A History of the River*
Copyright © 1993 by James Applewhite
Louisiana State University Press
Reprinted by permission of the author

Magnolia Tree
Copyright © 1997 by
Roger Winstead

adopted on a sweeping scale, has resulted in a dramatic diminishing of the "front-porch visiting" that strengthened communities and long characterized the South.

Moreover, even in the Carolinas' Golden Age, some places are in trouble. Job creation has been more rapid in urban than in rural areas; and the rural church, the rural school, and other small-town institutions have been subjected to severe economic stress resulting from a decline in the tobacco industry, a diminishing of quality job opportunities, and a depopulation of rural counties. Fewer people live in rural settings than in metropolitan places.

At least three metropolitan areas have more than one million residents: Charlotte/Gastonia/Rock Hill; Greensboro/Winston-Salem/High Point, and Raleigh/Durham/Chapel Hill. The Greenville/Spartanburg/Anderson metro is nearing a million.

Fueled by their metro areas, North Carolina and South Carolina have experienced robust population growth, especially since 1970. Among the states, North Carolina ranks 11th with 7.5 million people, South Carolina 26th with 3.7 million. But the volume of growth is only one dimension of a richer story.

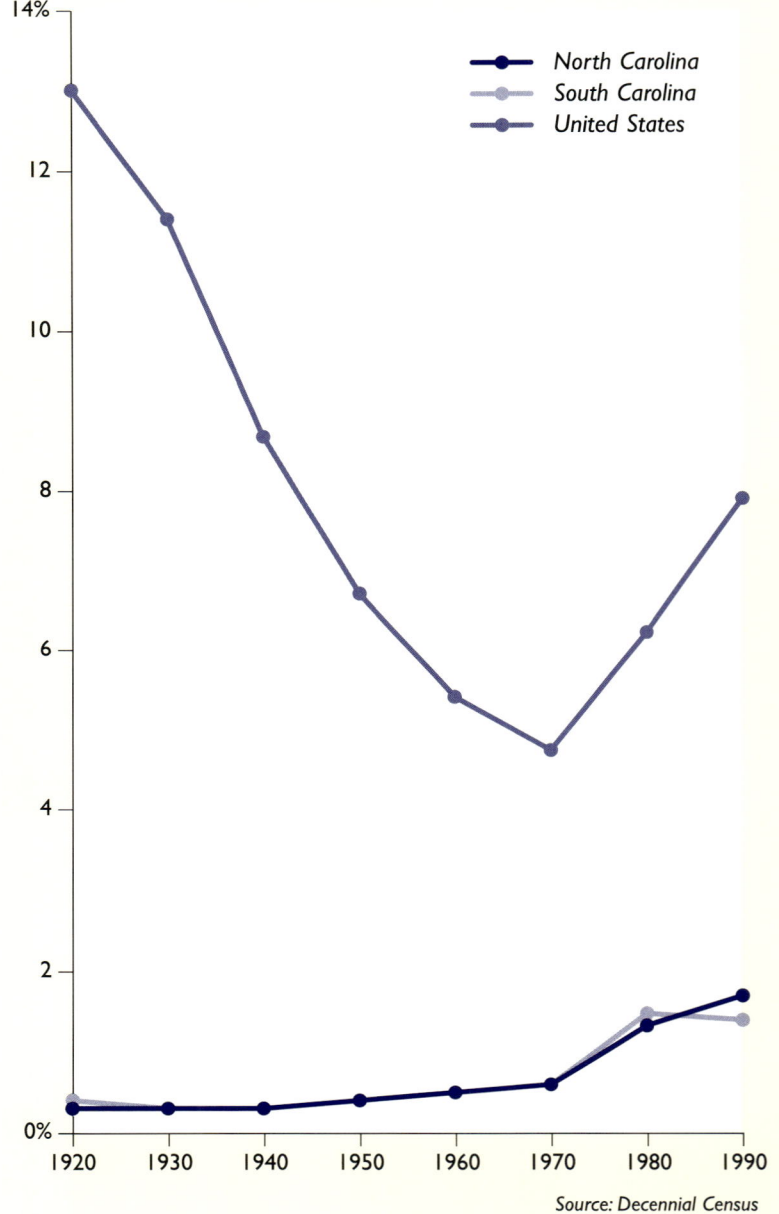

Diversity on the Rise
Percent of residents foreign-born — NC, SC, and U.S., 1920-1990

Source: Decennial Census

You're not from around here, are you?

Our states have become population importers — of blacks and whites, Latinos and Asians from every section of the country and from abroad. The story of today's Carolinas, as MDC told it in the 1998 *State of the South*, can't be captured only in black and white, but in Technicolor™.

Many thousands of blacks left the region during the mid-century's great out-migration. South Carolina switched from a majority-black to a majority-white state before the 1930 Census. And now many blacks are returning home — the black population rising by 13 percent in North Carolina since 1990, by 9.5 percent in South Carolina.

In addition to seeing a reversal of black migration patterns, the Carolinas have also experienced a turnabout in the "brain drain." Now, like the rest of the seaboard South, the two states attract more of the highly educated, whites as well as blacks. In the aggregate, newly arrived residents have higher education attainment than the people already living in the region.

In the 1990s, North Carolina has outpaced South Carolina in attracting new residents from other states. North Carolina had net domestic migration of 430,000, South Carolina 91,000. One way to measure the influence of population shifts is to look at voting patterns: In the past two statewide elections, nearly one out of five people who cast ballots in North Carolina had lived in the state for no more than six years.

Unlike the 1920s, when waves of immigrants entered the United States and settled in the Northeast and Midwest while the Carolinas remained isolated, the immigration and domestic migration patterns of the 1990s have begun to transform the South. In search of jobs, Latinos

Growing Faster than the Nation
Percent increase in population by race/ethnicity, 1990-1997

	Total Population	Hispanic	White	Black	American Indian	Asian
United States	7.29%	30.00%	3.18%	10.86%	11.97%	32.75%
South	10.26%	33.28%	5.99%	15.05%	10.74%	48.47%
North Carolina	11.54%	72.05%	9.39%	13.23%	18.00%	60.02%
South Carolina	7.47%	25.69%	6.08%	9.48%	3.38%	29.40%

Source: U.S. Census Bureau

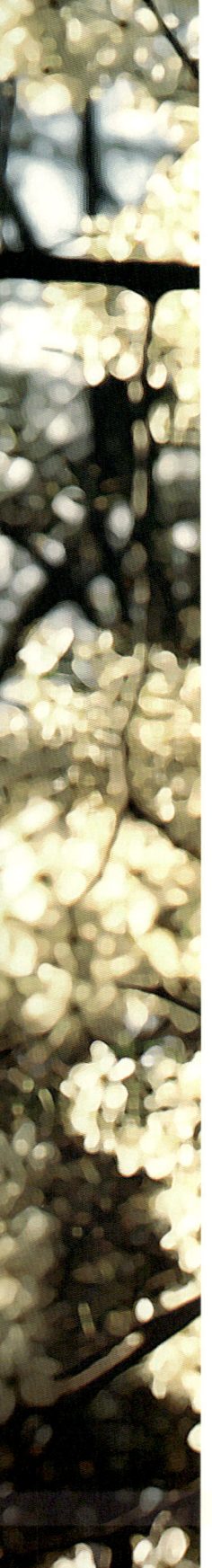

have moved up from Mexico and the Caribbean through Texas and Florida and into the Carolinas.

As a whole, the Hispanic population of the South increased by 33 percent since 1990. North Carolina's Hispanic population growth rate of 72 percent far exceeded that of the South, while South Carolina had a 25 percent growth in Hispanics.

Asians have also found job opportunities in the South, especially in cities. Over the past decade, the Asian population in North Carolina has grown 60 percent, in South Carolina 30 percent. By 1996, more than 14,000 Asians lived in both Wake County and Mecklenburg County; and among counties nationwide that began the decade with at least 2,000 Asians, these two North Carolina counties ranked in the top 15 in rate of growth of Asian population.

Were it not for the growth of black and Hispanic populations in the Carolinas, the region would be looking at an aging resident workforce with significantly fewer well-trained young adults in the pipeline to fill the needs of a healthy economy over the next decade and a half. North Carolina is projected to have 150,000 fewer whites aged 20 to 44 in the year 2015 than it has now, but the Tar Heel State will have 54,000 more blacks and 14,000 more Latinos in that age bracket. Similarly, South Carolina is expected to have 91,000 fewer 20- to 44-year-old whites in 2015, while the number of blacks increases by 3,000 and Latinos by 7,000.

"On the Great Migration"

An excerpt from *The Water is Wide* by Pat Conroy

In the parable of Yamacraw there was a time when the black people supported themselves well, worked hard, and lived up to the sacred tenets laid down in the Protestant ethic. Each morning the strong young men would take to their bateaux and search the shores and inlets for the large clusters of oysters, which the women and old men in the factory shucked into large jars. Yamacraw oysters were world famous. An island legend claims that a czar of Russia once ordered Yamacraw oysters for an imperial banquet. The white people propagate this rumor. The blacks, for the most part, would not know a czar from a fiddler crab, but the oysters were good, and the oyster factories operating on the island provided a substantial living for all the people. Everyone worked and everyone made money. Then a villain appeared. It was an industrial factory situated on a knoll above

Depending on older workers

Still, the overall aging of the population represents a critical trend in the Carolinas. North Carolina is expected to have half a million more people 65 and older in 2015 than now, South Carolina a quarter of a million more. The burgeoning postretirement population has important consequences in housing and health care, in retail and recreation, in social insurance and social services.

But there will be an even bigger bulge in 2015, a bulge that has consequences for governments, nonprofits, and businesses. In 2015, North Carolina is expected to have in excess of one million more people — including 725,000 whites, 250,000 blacks — aged 45 to 64 than it has now. South Carolina will have 460,000 more, including 313,000 whites and 140,000 blacks.

Oyster Pickers
Jonathan Green, 1990
Oil on Canvas
47" x 98"
Collection of Drs. Yele and Shirley Aluko

the Savannah River many miles away from Yamacraw. The villain spewed its excrement into the river, infected the creeks, and as silently as the pull of the tides, the filth crept to the shores of Yamacraw.... Someone took samples of the water around Yamacraw, analyzed them under a microscope, and reported the results to the proper officials. Soon after this, little white signs were placed by the oyster banks forbidding anyone to gather the oysters. Ten thousand oysters were now as worthless as grains of sand....

Since a factory is soulless and faceless, it could not be moved to understand the destruction its coming had wrought. When the oysters became contaminated, the island's only industry folded almost immediately. The great migration began.

From *The Water is Wide*
Copyright © 1972 by Pat Conroy
Houghton Mifflin, Boston
Reprinted by permission of the author

THE STATE OF THE CAROLINAS

Aging of the Workforce
Projected population change (in thousands) — NC and SC, 1995-2015

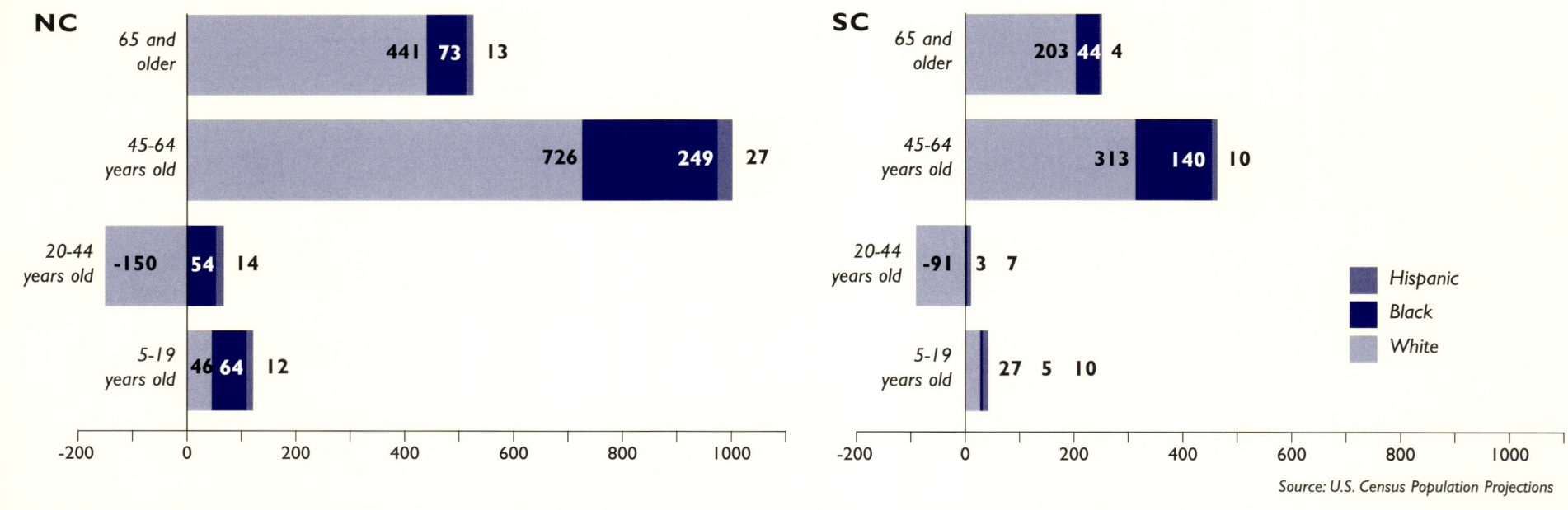

Source: U.S. Census Population Projections

This bulge results from the post-World War II baby boom. Almost all of the working members of that generation will still be in the workforce of the Carolinas during the next 15 years. Most public policy debate looks ahead to when baby boomers begin retiring, but policymakers thinking about the workforce in our states can't ignore baby boomers before they retire.

It's difficult to generalize about an entire generation. Many baby boomers are as well educated and as well-off as their counterparts in other regions. But the Carolinas, like their sister Southern states, have a larger-than-average share of baby boomers who grew up with inadequate schools, who were trained for an agricultural or low-skill industrial economy, who remember black-and-white TV and tremble at the thought of working on a computer. The Carolinas' economy will remain heavily dependent on these aging workers as it speeds into the new century, and the two states will have the task of ensuring the availability of adult education and retraining to enhance the skills of the people in the baby boom bulge.

Diversifying economy, proliferating jobs

As a modernizer, James Buchanan Duke specifically intended to transform the economy of the Carolinas. He did so by investing in the generation of hydroelectric power. Indeed, he helped set in motion a dynamic that has reshaped this region over and over again.

In the 1920s, farming and light manufacturing provided the jobs for seven out of 10 employed persons in the two states. Now, however, agriculture directly accounts for no more than 5 percent of the states' employment. And, while North Carolina and South Carolina today have a larger share of their workers in manufacturing than the nation as a whole, factory work accounts for fewer than 30 percent of employed persons.

Diversity, that long-sought goal, has become a reality.

There is diversity in agriculture. North Carolina remains the nation's leading tobacco-growing state. But within North Carolina, tobacco now ranks third, behind hogs and poultry, in annual cash receipts.

There is diversity in manufacturing. By the mid-1970s, seven upstate counties of South Carolina were home to more than 200 international firms from 18 countries. While the traditional manufacturing enterprises of textiles, cigarettes, and furniture remain powerful sectors of the Carolinas' economy, the states are moving briskly to a base of high-value-added manufacturing — ranging from automobiles to pharmaceuticals to electronic equipment.

And there is diversity throughout the economy. Increasingly, the people of the Carolinas are working in offices, providing services, and competing in the global economy. A ranking of the top 10 industries in North Carolina in 1996 placed real estate first, health services second, chemicals third, and construction fourth. Both Carolinas have moved well into the service sector, with many of the sector's jobs providing high-value services and paying high wages.

As a result, the overall income of Carolinians has improved markedly. Seven decades ago, per capita personal income in both states was less than half the national level. Now, North Carolina has risen to 90 percent of national per capita income, with South Carolina at about 80 percent.

In contrast to the 1920s, when our two states were more economically isolated, America's roaring '90s did not bypass the Carolinas.

Starting in the mid-'90s, jobs grew and unemployment fell, even as our states' traditional industries continued to shrink. The Carolinas approach the end of the century with an economy characterized by considerable churning: on one day, state and federal agencies bring news of a further surge in hiring; on another day, an old, established company announces a round of layoffs.

In manufacturing, for example, North Carolina had a 38 percent decline in employment in tobacco products and a 19 percent decline in textiles from 1988 to 1996. At the same time, employment in industrial machinery rose 31 percent and electrical equipment went up by 9 percent. And job growth in services (68 percent), retail trade (22 percent), and finance/insurance/

From Farming and Forestry...

Industry distribution — 1920

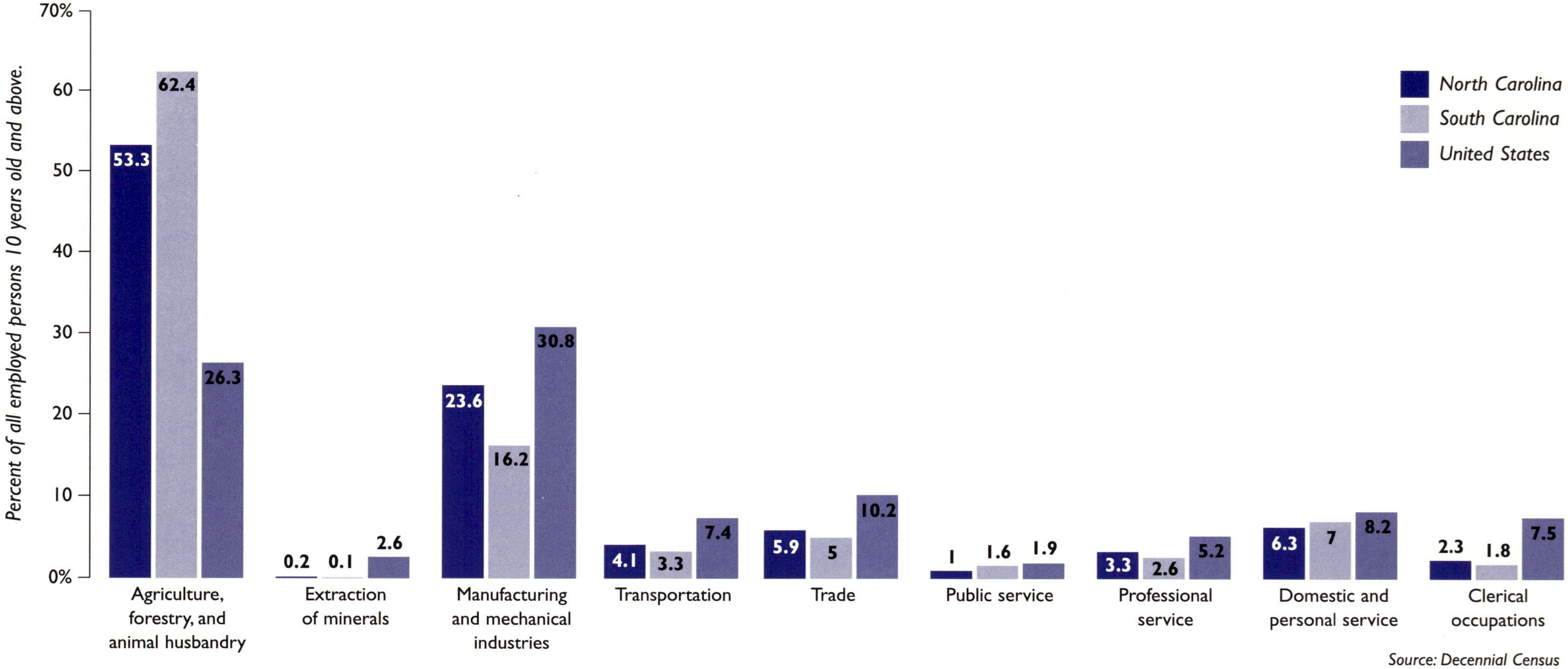

Industry	North Carolina	South Carolina	United States
Agriculture, forestry, and animal husbandry	53.3	62.4	26.3
Extraction of minerals	0.2	0.1	2.6
Manufacturing and mechanical industries	23.6	16.2	30.8
Transportation	4.1	3.3	7.4
Trade	5.9	5	10.2
Public service	1	1.6	1.9
Professional service	3.3	2.6	5.2
Domestic and personal service	6.3	7	8.2
Clerical occupations	2.3	1.8	7.5

Percent of all employed persons 10 years old and above.

Source: Decennial Census

real estate (24 percent) outpaced the emerging manufacturing industries. The economic transition of the late 1990s, therefore, offers many Carolinians wider opportunities, and it presents some of them with uncertainty and thus heightened anxieties.

As the 1990s came to a close, North Carolina, the larger of the two states, clearly had the more robust economy. *State Policy Reports* publishes an economic momentum index, combining one-year shifts in employment, personal income, and population. The most recent index had North Carolina ranked sixth in the nation, with growth above the national average; and South Carolina ranked 27th, with growth somewhat below the national average.

...To Manufacturing and Services
Industry distribution — 1990

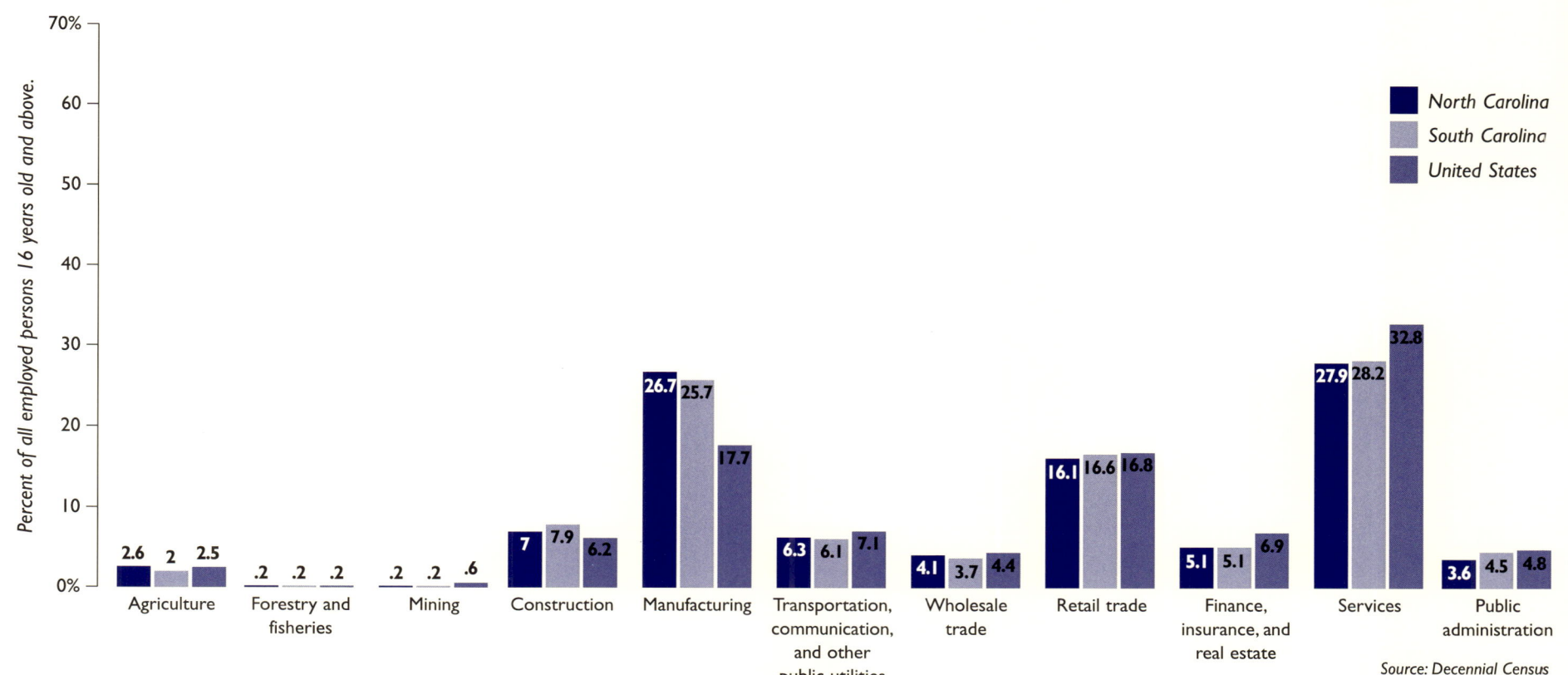

Source: Decennial Census

Incomes on the Rise...

Average per capita personal income — 1929 and 1996 (in 1996 dollars)

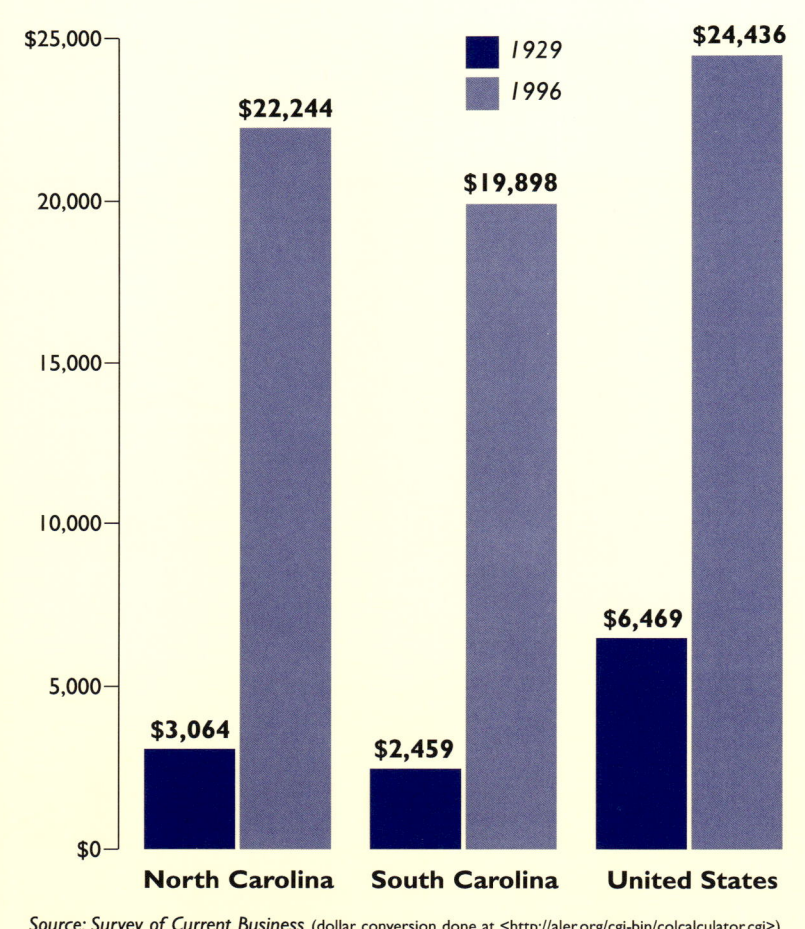

Source: *Survey of Current Business* (dollar conversion done at <http://aler.org/cgi-bin/colcalculator.cgi>)

...And Catching up with the Nation

Average per capita personal income — as a percent of U.S., 1929–1996

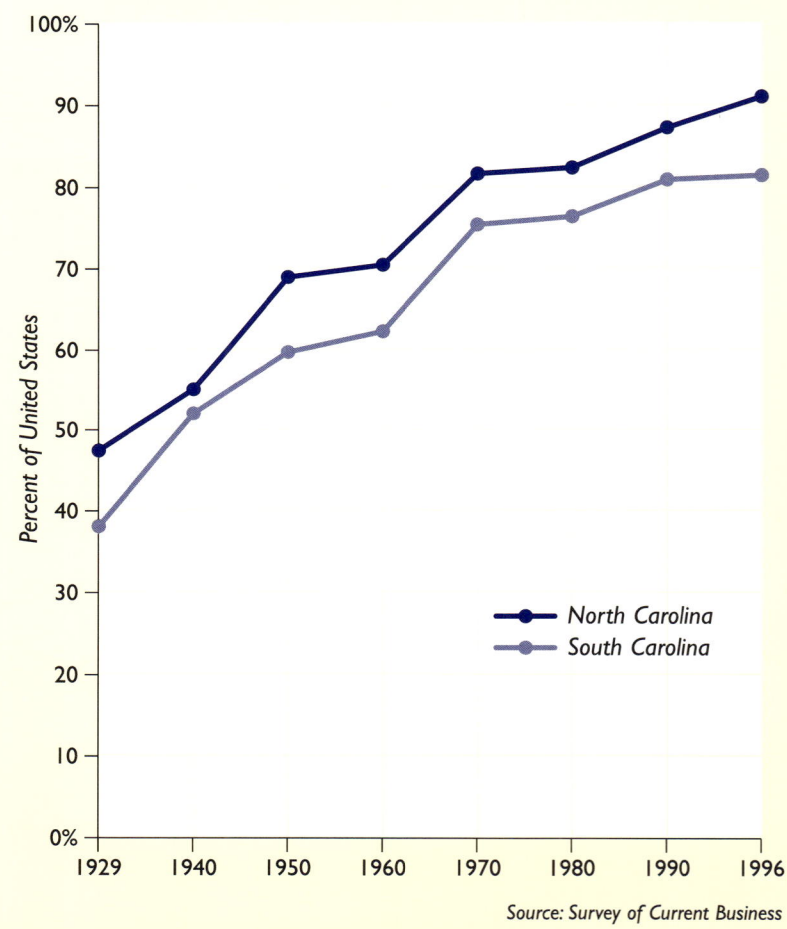

Source: *Survey of Current Business*

Gains, but not enough

For two decades or more, education has been regarded as the Achilles' heel of the Carolinas, and of the South generally. Low educational attainment rates were seen as stumbling blocks to our states' economic advancement — and with some justification.

Indeed, for much of this century, when our region advertised itself as a place of cheap land and cheap labor, too many Carolinians saw little value in education beyond a year or two in high school. After all, steady, albeit low-wage, jobs in fields or factories beckoned.

But even those who persist in reminding our states of their vulnerability in the face of the economy's demand for higher levels of knowledge and schooling can hardly ignore the sweeping changes — and advances — that North Carolina and South Carolina have made in education. James Buchanan Duke gave expression to the value he saw in higher education by transforming a small college in Durham into a major international university, as well as investing in three other private colleges in the Carolinas. Now, the two states have a broad network of both public and private universities, which create an intellectual synergy and which, together, provide a platform for further economic and societal advancement.

Furthermore, the Carolinas have taken important policy and programmatic steps that amount to surgery on that Achilles' heel. They have repositioned community colleges as critical elements of strategies to modernize their industrial bases and diversify their economies. Bursts of reform in public elementary and secondary schools have, over time, resulted in gains in achievement. And now, South Carolina has begun to follow the lead of North Carolina in focusing on the imperatives of early childhood development to bolster preparation for attainment in school.

North Carolina's Research Triangle Park derives sustenance from the presence of three world-class research universities, one at each point of the triangle. And South Carolina could not have attracted such transforming international investment to Greenville/Spartanburg without the significant training opportunities afforded by its technical colleges.

Graduation gap erased

For much of this century, the education challenge in the Carolinas centered on a clear target: close the gap between our states and the nation in high school graduation. While too many young people still drop out without a diploma in hand, the Carolinas have largely succeeded in hitting the once-elusive target.

Measured in terms of adults 25 years and older, North Carolina and South Carolina have greatly narrowed the gap with the nation in high school graduation. In North Carolina, 76 percent of adults have graduated from high school, and in South Carolina 74 percent — compared to the U.S. at 82 percent. That some gap persists is attributable to the large number of older Southern adults who grew up in the old, low-skill economy.

Look at younger adults, and a more telling picture emerges. Among North Carolinians between age 25 and 44, fully 88.7 percent had a high school diploma in 1998, above the national level of 88 percent. South Carolina trailed, but barely, at 85.3 percent.

The influx of well-educated newcomers explains some, but surely not all, of this progress.

Scores on the National Assessment of Education Progress tests show that North Carolina and South Carolina still fall behind the nation in achievement — but not as far as they would have a decade or two ago. In eighth-grade math proficiency scores in 1996, North Carolina's average of 268 fell only three points below the national average of 271, and South

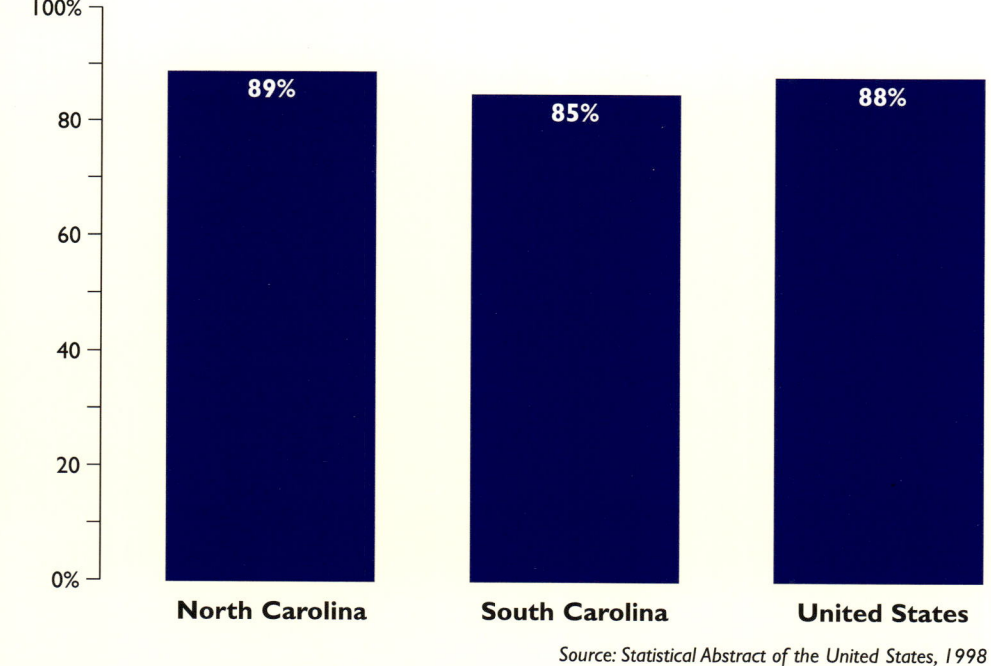

Matching the Nation in High School Grads
Percent of population aged 25-44 with at least a high school diploma, March 1998

- North Carolina: 89%
- South Carolina: 85%
- United States: 88%

Source: Statistical Abstract of the United States, 1998

Carolina was 10 points back at 261. On the science proficiency tests, the North Carolina average of 147 was only one point lower than the nation's; the South Carolina average of 139 put it nine points lower.

While persisting in the quest to overcome the long historic lag in elementary and secondary education, North Carolina and South Carolina have to confront an issue that is difficult to quantify. In far too many schools, especially in inner cities and rural areas, low expectations, on the part of both teachers and students, deprive our states of the full blossoming of potential talent. The Carolinas have much more to do to instill a spirit of high expectations and to provide the resources required to meet high expectations — and to the extent that they do so, measurements of achievement and accountability will surely rise.

From diplomas to degrees

Even as the Carolinas work to preserve and extend their gains in education up to the 12th grade, the states face new demands, rooted in demographic and economic change, to bolster higher education. Although the states are catching up with the nation in high school attainment, they still lag significantly in college-going — at precisely the moment when education beyond high school has become a prerequisite for a middle-class standard of living. Twenty-five years ago, according to *The Economist*, college graduates earned 58 percent more than high school graduates; now college graduates earn 77 percent more.

The imperative is not only economic but also civic. The health of our democracy requires

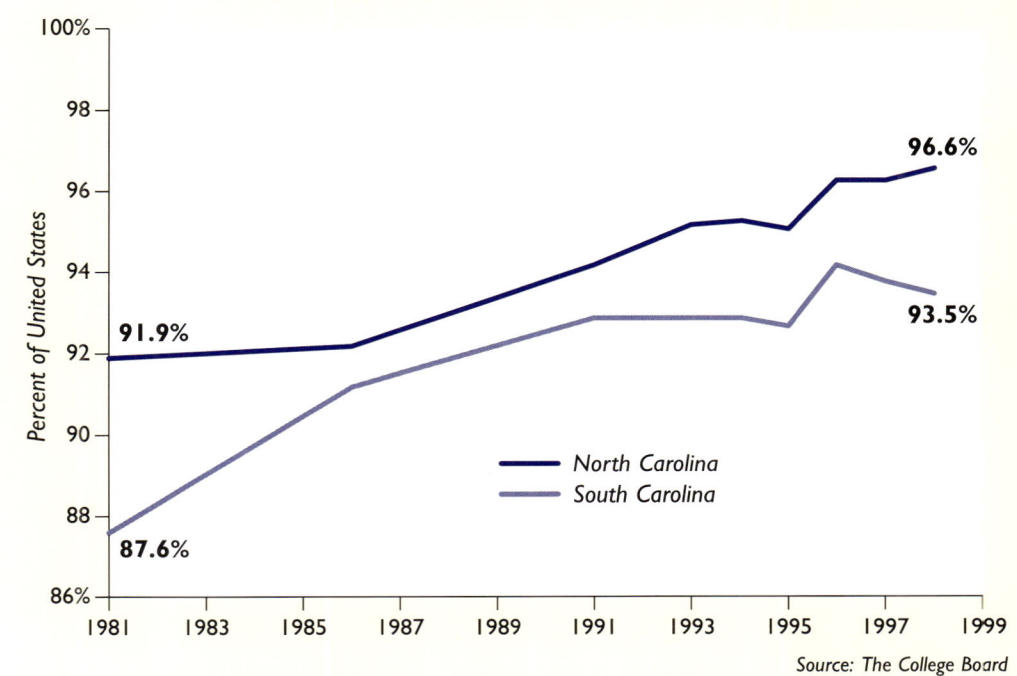

Progress with Room for Improvement
NC and SC average SAT scores as a percent of the U.S. average

Source: The College Board

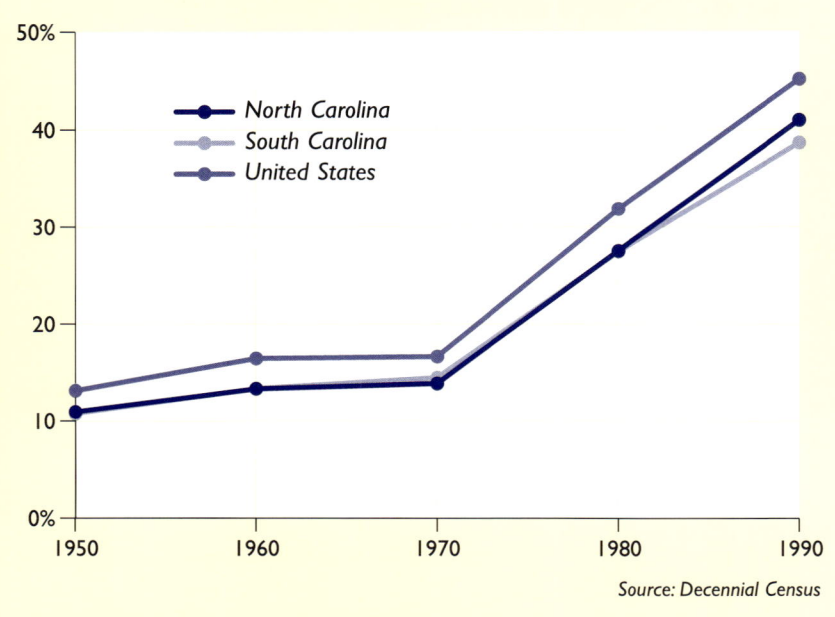

College Attendance on the Rise, but Not Enough

Percent of NC, SC, and U.S. residents with at least some college

Source: Decennial Census

and universities, eight independent colleges and universities, and 16 technical community colleges.

Together, these are major assets and are crucial to preparing for an economy in which the transfer of knowledge will outpace the production of goods. This means significantly increasing the number of people who go on to 13, 14, and more years of education. The growing demand on our colleges and universities will come not only from the looming growth in the college-age population but also from our states' need for aggressive action to educate even more of their citizens for the economy of the 21st century.

The Mortensen Research Seminar in Iowa recently produced a detailed analysis of college-going and found that a 19-year-old's chances of being enrolled in college varied widely among the states. Its index was based on a formula that combined high school graduation rates and college continuation rates to give the "best estimate of the proportion of each state's 19-year-olds that were enrolled in college in the fall of 1996." Under the Mortensen formula for "chance for college by age 19," both North Carolina and South Carolina fall below the national level. North Carolina ranked 42nd, South Carolina 43rd.

citizens who have the skills to participate and the knowledge to make informed decisions.

The march of time has proved Mr. Duke a visionary in his insistence on higher education of the highest quality. He put his money into private institutions, and the people of the two states have invested strongly in extensive, accessible systems of public colleges and universities. Now, North Carolina has 16 public universities, 36 independent colleges and universities, and 58 community colleges. South Carolina has 18 public colleges

No longer a guy thing?

Men are less likely to go on to college than women. In both community colleges and universities, college-going among women is rising, while male enrollment is lagging. And once in college, men are less likely than women to graduate.

After noting that women have surpassed men in college continuation since the late 1980s, the Mortensen seminar authors wonder, "We keep asking: what's wrong with the guys?" It is a key question for the Carolinas. Women, it's clear, are adapting more readily than men to the requirements of the changing economy. And the challenge is to ensure that more men begin adapting, too.

Although blacks have made substantial gains in college attainment, our states still have an unacceptable gap between whites and blacks in education beyond high school. In both states, the proportion of white adults with a bachelor's degree or beyond far exceeds the proportion of black adults with a degree. Only 10 percent of black adults in South Carolina have a college degree, nearly 14 percent in North Carolina. Among white adults in both states, the proportion with a degree rises above 22 percent.

Eliminating differences in education attainment would shrink the earnings gap between black men and white men. Race still matters, but it matters less and less as more blacks and whites enter the workforce with a degree in hand. Closing this higher education gap, while reaching for even higher percentages of both whites and blacks with college-level education, would give the Carolinas at least two beneficial results: an increased supply of talent and an amelioration of racial frictions.

Just as a long-ago educational leader, quoted by the historian George Tindall, warned the South that it was in "grave danger of ballyhooing

The New Gender Gap
Women as a percentage of total students enrolled*

North Carolina, Fall 1998	
NC Community College System**	59%
NC Public University System	55.9%

South Carolina, Fall 1997	
SC Technical Education System	57.4%
SC Public Universities	55.4%

United States, Fall 1996	
Public 2-year Institutions	57.6%
Public 4-year Institutions	54.4%

Most recent figures available for each category
**Curriculum students*
Source: State Data Sources and Digest of Education Statistics

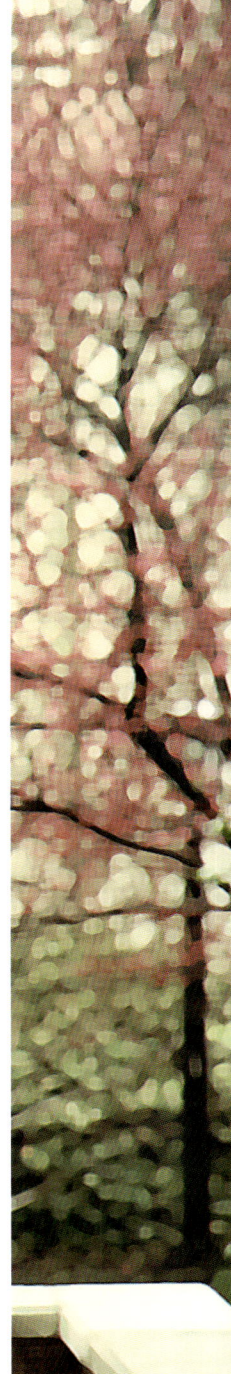

itself into further backwardness," today's Carolinas' leaders risk sliding into complacency. Too much ballyhooing about progress in elementary and secondary schools — and especially about the quality of our community colleges and universities — and our states will learn anew the danger of resting on laurels.

Two realities for families and children

The 75 years since Mr. Duke created The Endowment have brought a sea change in the condition of children and families — and in the way society cares for its young. In the 1920s, divorce was rare. Many children in the Carolinas worked at a gainful job, not only older adolescents but also 25 percent of the 10- to 15-year-olds. Then, it was deeply humanitarian for Mr. Duke to invest in and to upgrade orphanages to care for children — regardless of race — who lost one or both parents.

Now, most children growing up in North Carolina and South Carolina have vastly brighter prospects — enormously broader horizons — than those of their counterparts of seven decades ago. In the Golden Age at the end of the 1990s, there is no rampant child labor, no Great Depression, neither civil war nor world war that will take their fathers, or even many of them, away.

To try to assess the needs of children and families today is to come to grips with interlocking trends, modern circumstances, and new knowledge; it is difficult to generalize. Still, to look at families and children in the Carolinas is to see two overarching realities. For the majority, life has never been as good as it is at the dawn of the 21st century. A substantial minority, however, remains at risk economically, socially, and emotionally.

The Kids Count project of the Annie E. Casey Foundation has devised an index for determining the segment of the population of children living in "high risk" families. Such children are defined as having four of the following six characteristics: not living with two parents, living in a family with income below the poverty line, having a head-of-household who is a high school dropout, living with parents without steady employment, lacking health insurance, and receiving welfare benefits. According to Kids Count, 19 percent of South Carolina children fall into the "high risk" category, above the national average of 14 percent. North Carolina fell slightly below the national average with 13 percent of children at "high risk."

Two parents, two workers

The robust economy of the 1990s has produced a spurt of new, higher-paying jobs in the Carolinas, offering millions of families opportunity for a higher standard of living. And yet, even in a more diverse economy, many families rely on two incomes to maintain what they now regard as a middle-class standard of living. The modern consumer-economy, resting on a lot of debt, has heightened expectations and raised the level of material possessions. As expectations have increased, women have streamed into the workforce, many out of economic necessity, many out of career choice, some out of both.

But, of course, our two states have a long history of women deeply engaged in the workforce. In states with a large base of low-wage manufacturing and farming, families depended on two incomes to hold themselves together economically. In many mill villages, dad worked one shift, mom worked another.

Thus, the legacy of history and the dynamics of the modern economy result in the Carolinas having a higher level of mothers at work than the United States as a whole.

The Women

by Michael Chitwood

They don't stitch
Bible verses into cloth squares
to decorate sitting-room walls.
They keep their sayings with them,
in the weave room and cloth room,
by the doors of Drawing-In,
at the window to Supply.

They don't have to back up to take their pay.
If you're looking for a fight,
they'll help you find it.
They've got another shift to pull when they get home.
Women work daylight and graveyard
all their lives,
and sometimes do it pregnant.

They're the ones, after Revelations,
who fill in the blanks.

"The Women" by Michael Chitwood
From *The Weave Room*
Copyright © 1998 by Michael Chitwood
University of Chicago Press
Reprinted by permission of the author

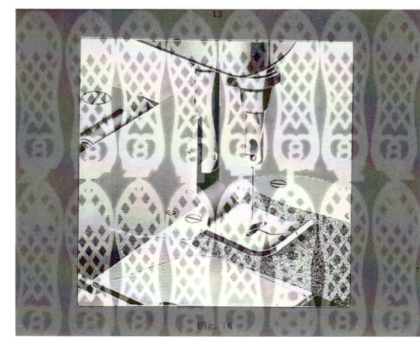

Machine Tender
Phil Moody, 1994
Cibachrome and Silver prints
62" x 24"

Nationally, about 75 percent of mothers with children ages 6 to 17 are in the labor force, and about 60 percent of mothers with children under age 6. In North Carolina, about 78 percent of mothers with children ages 6 to 17 are working, and 67 percent with children under age 6. In South Carolina, about 80 percent of mothers with children 6 to 17 and 67 percent with children under age 6 are in the labor force.

For many young children, the prevalence of two-worker families means several hours a day under the supervision of nonfamily caregivers — or under no supervision at all. For many school-age children, the result is hours at home in front of a TV, video game, or Internet hookup. For some teenagers, the hours of late afternoon and early evening have become the time for crime, drugs, and sex.

In effect, thousands of children are left "orphaned" for several hours day-to-day.

Consequently, in both states, the public demand has risen for high-quality day care and for extended-day programs in the schools.

Adding intensity to these issues are research findings with respect to early childhood development and to the effect of television, music, and movies on the attitudes and behavior of preteens and teenagers. Brain-scanning research has revealed that richly stimulating experiences between birth and 4 years of age are crucial for mental development. An array of research has suggested that violence and other crudity in mass entertainment have raised the level of antisocial behavior among young people.

Thus, concern over the well-being of children and the condition of their families revolves around both their economic status and the influence of the surrounding culture. Of special concern are the afternoon orphans.

Poverty of body, and spirit

Despite the robust economy, troubling societal trends have left hundreds of thousands of Carolinas' children and their families economically vulnerable and deprived of hope. A combination of cultural and economic forces bear down on today's vulnerable families in such a way as to conspire to rob many children of the support and attention they need for healthy development.

The troubling trends include:

- A poverty rate among children higher than the rate among adults.
- A two-decade proliferation of single-parent families.
- An epidemic of parental alcohol and drug addiction that has led to a dramatic increase in neglected and abused children.

In terms of overall poverty, North Carolina and South Carolina fell below the national poverty rate in the mid-1990s. From a historical perspective, this is an amazing achievement. But the drop in the Carolinas' poverty rates does not indicate a recent drop in the absolute number of poor people, but rather an expansion in the numbers of middle-class and affluent people living in the two states.

Most significantly, it doesn't mean a decline in the number of children living in poverty. Of the 885,000 poor North Carolinians in 1996, fully 337,000 were children. Of the 482,000 poor South Carolinians, 184,000 were children.

Of course, whether children suffer from poverty has less to do with their own efforts and ambitions than with the circumstances of their parents and related adults. Of North Carolina's

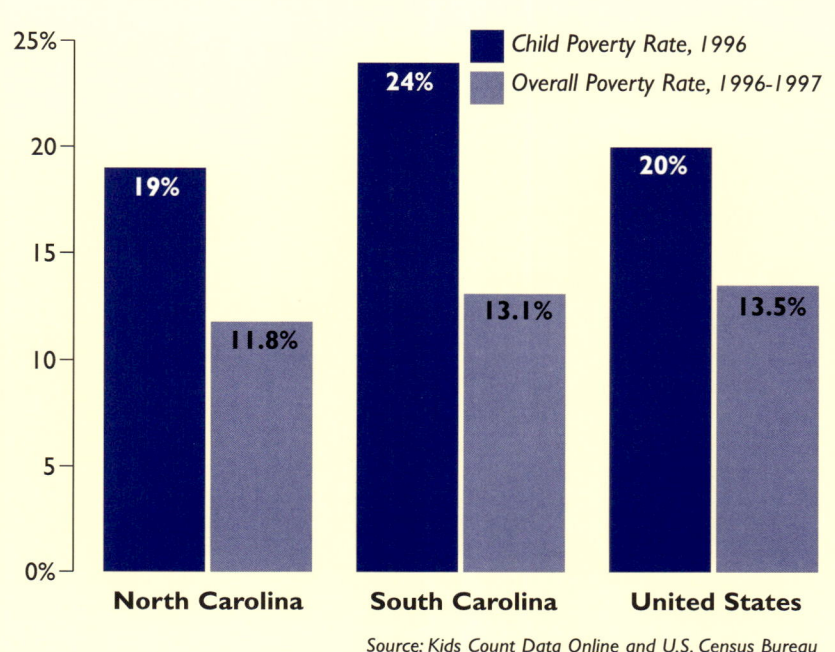

Poor Children, Poor Future
Percentage of children living in poverty and percentage of total population living in poverty

	Child Poverty Rate, 1996	Overall Poverty Rate, 1996-1997
North Carolina	19%	11.8%
South Carolina	24%	13.1%
United States	20%	13.5%

Source: Kids Count Data Online and U.S. Census Bureau

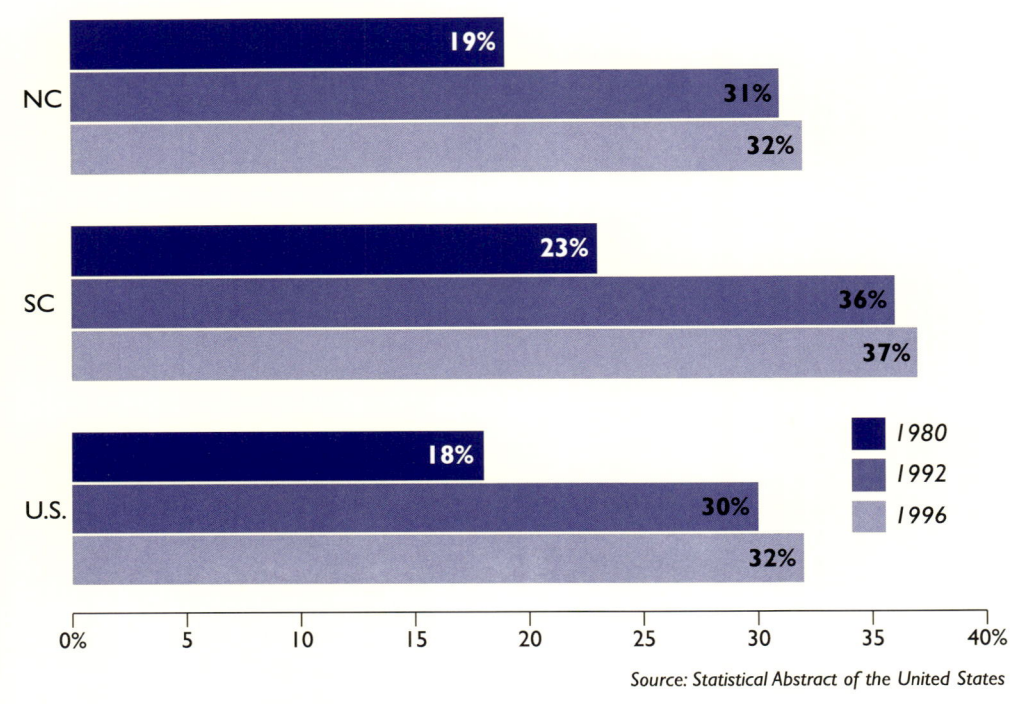

Surge in Single Parenthood

Births to unmarried women as a percent of all births — 1980, 1992, 1996

NC: 19% / 31% / 32%
SC: 23% / 36% / 37%
U.S.: 18% / 30% / 32%

Source: Statistical Abstract of the United States

1.9 million children, 19 percent are poor, 29 percent live in families with a single parent, and 15 percent lack health insurance. Of South Carolina's 955,000 children, 24 percent live in poverty, 31 percent reside with a single parent, and 17 percent lack health insurance.

Despite a sharp decline in teenage pregnancies in the 1990s, the Carolinas still must contend with the consequences of a surge in births to unmarried women — adults as well as teenagers — since 1980. In South Carolina, births to unmarried women as a percentage of all births jumped from about 23 percent in 1980 to 37 percent in 1996. North Carolina went from about 19 percent to 32 percent in that same period.

About one-fourth of families today are headed by a single parent, most of them women (but an increasing number of men). Consider the triple disadvantage of a single mother: statistically, she is likely to have no more than a high school education, her earnings are likely to be less than a man's, and she must support her children on only one income. In the aggregate, among both blacks and whites, a vast economic divide separates two-parent families (especially those with two earners) and single-parent families.

Several shifts in societal attitudes — and, as a consequence, government policies — define the differences in the care of children in Mr. Duke's day and in today's Carolinas.

During the Great Depression, the nation adopted a policy of providing financial aid to families with dependent children. More recently, the nation has moved away from its half-century welfare strategy to a working-poor strategy. The welfare strategy assumes that single mothers would remain at home with children; the working-poor strategy seeks to insert poor parents into the workforce as quickly as possible, and it presumes that day care for young children and after-school supervision for older children will be available.

In addition, in cases in which children are removed from the homes of their birth-parents or close relatives, there has been a shift from orphanages to foster care and adoption. Foster care includes a range of short-term living arrangements, including placement in group homes or with an unrelated family. Public policy emphasizes the preservation of safe and stable families. But — whether stemming from the stress of economic deprivation, from alcohol or drug abuse, or from inadequate preparation for parenting — the Carolinas have experienced a sharp decade-long rise in the numbers of children moved into foster care.

From the mid-1980s through the first half of the 1990s, the rate of increase in the number of children entering the foster care system in our two states far surpassed the national rate. North Carolina had a 78 percent increase from 1990 to 1995, and South Carolina a 59 percent increase — both well above the national increase of 19 percent. Since the mid-'90s, the number of children going into foster care has stabilized, but at such an increased level that the system is under stress.

Black children tend to be removed from their homes at a somewhat higher rate than white children. In 1997-98, North Carolina had nearly 6,300 black children, 5,500 white children, and about 400 children of other races in foster care.

Foster Care

Children in foster care by race — NC (1998) and SC (1997-1998)

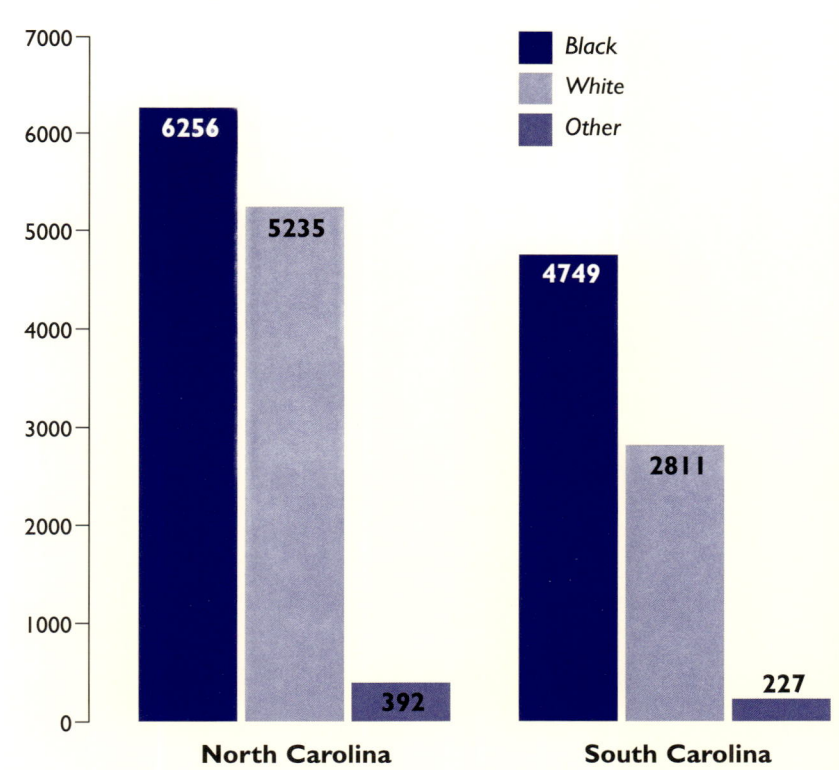

Source: North Carolina Division of Social Services, Fiscal Research Division; and South Carolina Department of Social Services

Black children also tend to remain in foster care for a longer duration than white children.

Of the more than 34,000 North Carolina children involved in substantiated cases of neglect and abuse in 1997-98, about 85 percent were classified as subject to neglect — and nearly 15 percent were judged victims of physical abuse. Half of the cases of substantiated neglect or abuse involved children 6 years of age or under.

Once again, it is difficult to generalize about a complex picture. Many children reap the benefits of a diligent social worker, of a caring foster parent, or of a well-run group home. And yet, overall, foster care is an imperfect solution. For many children, it means being shuffled from one place to another; for some, it means living in a household nearly as stressed or dysfunctional as the home from which they were removed. For more than one in four 18- to 21-year-olds no longer eligible for foster care, it means a spell of homelessness.

And, as social services officials know only too well, society has found no sure answers for that small segment of today's youth who are incorrigibly disruptive.

Two realities in health, too

Near the close of the 20th century, the Carolinas had a few isolated outbreaks of rubella, also known as German measles. The incidences occurred in communities where Latinos had recently arrived. The outbreaks made news in large part because rubella, especially dangerous in pregnant women, had been practically wiped

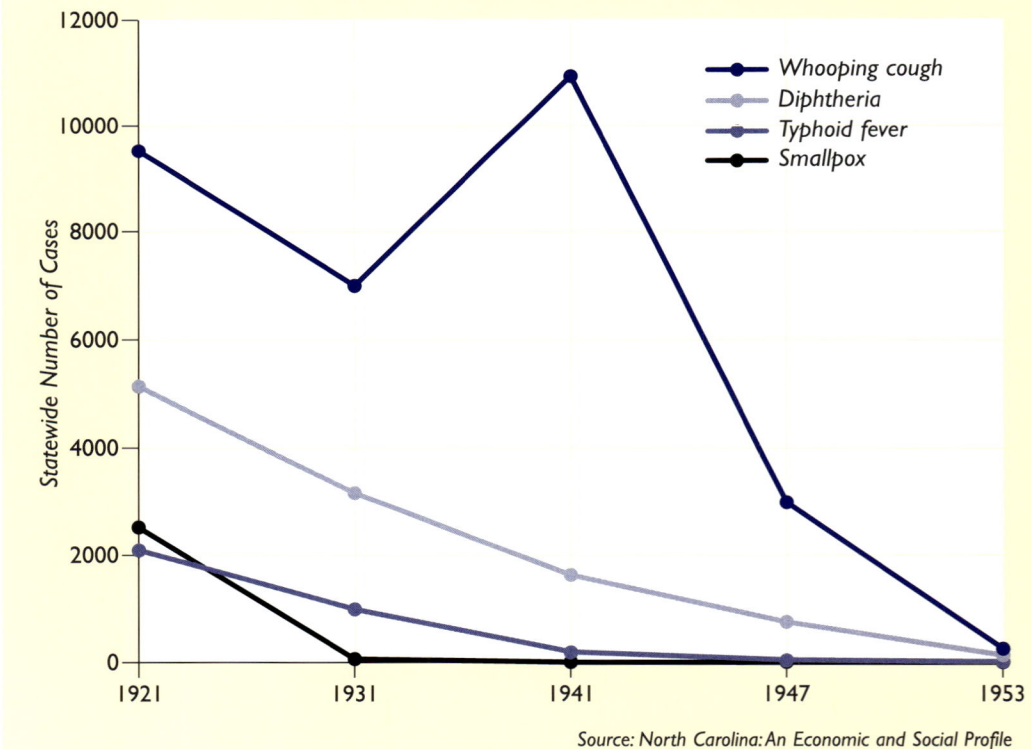

Vast Reduction in Old Diseases
Progress in prevention of some major illnesses in NC — 1921-1953

Source: North Carolina: An Economic and Social Profile

out in the United States. But the news was also that public health teams moved promptly to vaccinate the vulnerable and to stifle the spread of the disease.

One by one, diseases that were prevalent seven decades ago have been virtually eliminated or contained. Hardly anyone dies in the Carolinas now from typhoid fever or tuberculosis or pellagra. The rubella story illustrates both the advances of modern medicine and its extended reach into the small towns and hamlets of the Carolinas.

To a large extent, what Mr. Duke sought has been achieved. He gave The Endowment a mandate to spread hospitals across the rural landscape so that country people would have much the same access to health care that city people had. His vision anticipated and got a boost from the federal Hill-Burton Act. Seventy-five years after The Endowment was launched, geography no longer stands as an insurmountable barrier to quality health care.

By several health-care measurements, the people of North Carolina and South Carolina are substantially better off, in real terms and relative to the nation, than they were seven decades ago. In terms of physicians per 100,000 residents,

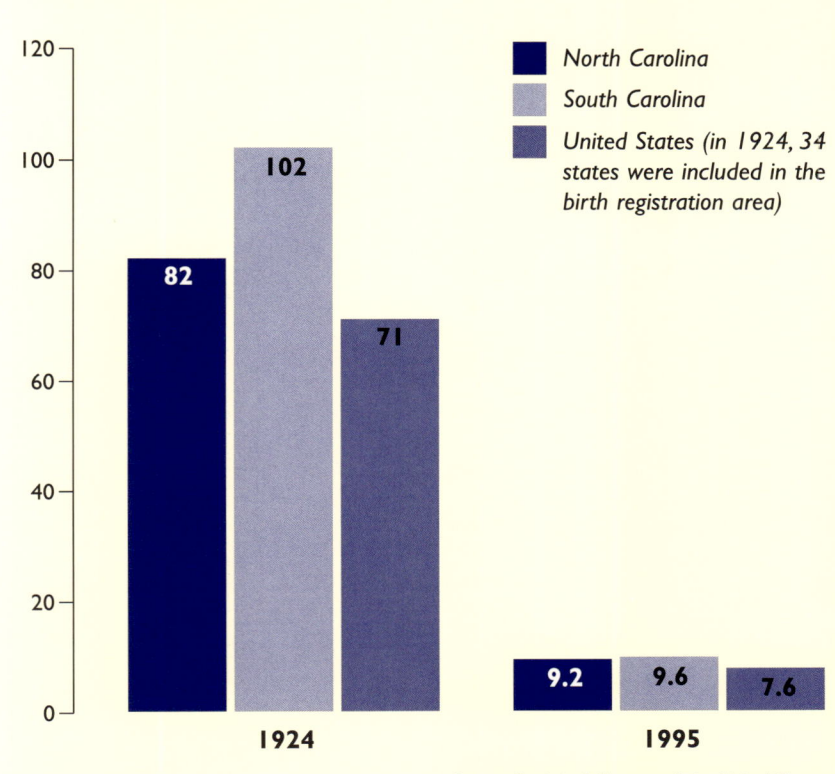

Way Down but Still Behind
Infant deaths per 1000 live births — 1924 and 1995

- North Carolina
- South Carolina
- United States (in 1924, 34 states were included in the birth registration area)

1924: 82, 102, 71
1995: 9.2, 9.6, 7.6

Source: Statistical Abstract of the United States

for example, our two states have narrowed the historic gap with the nation — but they still lag.

The plummeting of infant mortality over the course of the 20th century serves as an especially dramatic example. In the mid-'20s, there were more than 80 infant deaths per 1,000 live births in North Carolina, and more than 100 per 1,000 in South Carolina — both far above the national rate. In the mid-'90s, there were

9.2 infant deaths per 1,000 live births in North Carolina, 9.6 per 1,000 in South Carolina. While far below the levels of the 1920s, the infant mortality rates in our two states still exceed the national rate of 7.6. By today's standards, the Carolinas' infant mortality rates are still too high.

There remain, to be sure, distinct urban/rural differences in the distribution of health-care resources. It's still easier to attract a physician to a metropolitan area than to a small town, where he or she is likely to work longer hours and have few peers nearby. Many rural folks still must drive long distances to see a doctor or a nurse.

And yet, in addition to community hospitals, an array of initiatives and the proliferation of new technologies over the past three decades have dramatically lowered the barriers that long separated rural people from health care. Our states have rural health clinics with physician assistants and nurse practitioners who can link patients by electronic monitors to specialists many miles away. There are helicopter ambulances that ferry the gravely ill or injured to hospitals, and airplanes that fly doctors out to area health education centers.

Barrier defined in dollars

But if geography is less of a barrier to quality health care, economics stands out as a multi-dimensional barrier that separates the healthy from the not-so-healthy. Modern medical technology, which helps save many lives and heal many bodies, comes at a high, and seemingly ever-escalating, cost. More than 1.5 million people in our two states live in fear of an injury or an illness that may require medical care that they cannot afford.

In both North Carolina and South Carolina, the percentage of the population without health insurance is slightly below the national level of 15.4 percent. But lack of health coverage is an intensifying problem across the United States. Of the more than 40 million Americans without health insurance, North Carolina had 996,000 in 1995, South Carolina 546,000.

The people of the Carolinas rely less on health maintenance organizations than Americans in general. Our two states fall well below the national average in the percentage of their population enrolled in health maintenance organizations. Only 8.4 percent of South

Carolinians are in HMOs, nearly 15 percent of North Carolinians. Across the U.S., more than 26 percent are in HMOs.

In Mr. Duke's day, the challenge was to reach out the healing hand to rural people living far apart from each other. In today's Carolinas, the challenges are how to make the modern healing arts more affordable — and how to remove lingering differences in health status between whites and blacks.

In both of our states, African-Americans have an average life span of about four years fewer than whites. In North Carolina, according to a 1998 publication of the Office of Minority Health and the State Center for Health Statistics, black females die of heart disease, stroke, and diabetes at faster rates, adjusted for age, than white females. Similarly, black males have higher, age-adjusted rates of death from these maladies than white males.

The infant mortality rate among North Carolina blacks is 15.5 per 1,000 live births — eight percentage points above the white infant mortality rate.

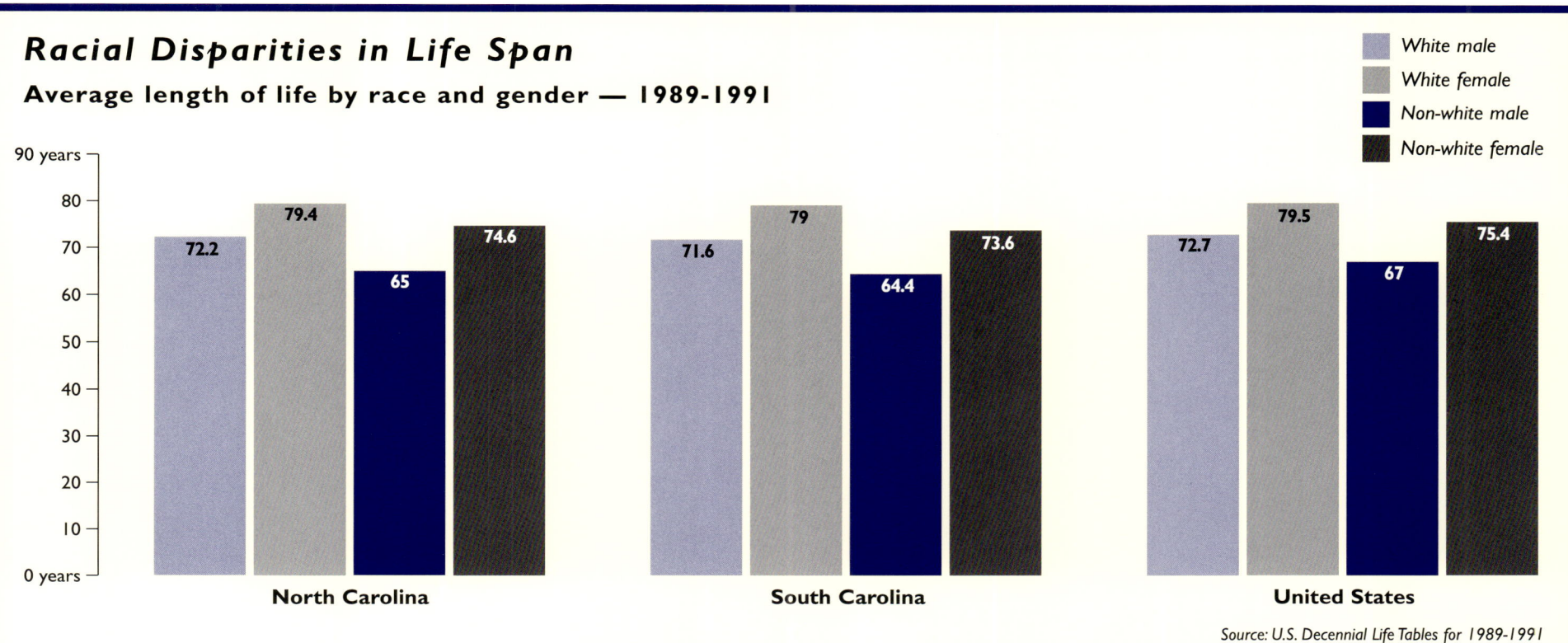

Racial Disparities in Life Span
Average length of life by race and gender — 1989-1991

Legend: White male, White female, Non-white male, Non-white female

North Carolina: 72.2, 79.4, 65, 74.6
South Carolina: 71.6, 79, 64.4, 73.6
United States: 72.7, 79.5, 67, 75.4

Source: U.S. Decennial Life Tables for 1989-1991

North Carolina and South Carolina rank below the national level in AIDS cases — though South Carolina's rate of 23.5 per 100,000 residents is only slightly below the national level of 25.6. The AIDS death rates are significantly higher for blacks than for whites — in 1996, for example, 16.2 deaths from AIDS per 100,000 black females in North Carolina and 59.4 deaths per 100,000 black males, contrasted with one death per 100,000 white females and 7.4 deaths per 100,000 white males.

In addition to overcoming the barrier of affordability and differences between races, the Carolinas face the difficult task of encouraging millions of people to shield themselves from ill health by altering their daily habits. After all, the health status of a population is not only a function of the availability and affordability of doctors, nurses, and hospitals, but also of people's lifestyles and day-to-day behavior. Prevention of disease stems from nutrition, physical exercise, and abstaining from harmful substances.

Nearly one in three residents of both North Carolina and South Carolina is overweight. About one in four adults smokes. And, according to the School of Public Health at the University of North Carolina at Chapel Hill, seven out of 10 North Carolina adults do not get adequate exercise.

Whatever the trends in individuals' daily habits, the economics of health-care delivery have created a powerful dynamic of change and dislocation at the close of the 20th century. An age of consolidation has overtaken hospitals, doctors' practices, and insurers. It is an age of considerable uncertainty for both the deliverers and the consumers of health care.

Consolidation has resulted in many hospitals owning health maintenance organizations as well as pulling groups of physicians under their institutional umbrellas. The trend has given hospital boards of directors increased power and new, though often unrecognized, responsibilities. In the 1920s, Mr. Duke thought the future quality of rural health care rested largely in propagating hospitals. These days, the resolution of health-care issues rests not only in the hands of public authorities but also, increasingly, in the hands of hospital boards — including the boards of for-profit corporations that have purchased many of the Carolinas' community hospitals.

Religion: trends and tension

In deciding to invest in rural Methodist churches, Mr. Duke acted from both personal devotion and broad societal vision. He sought to give back to the denomination that had given so much meaning in his own life. And, more, he saw in religion a critical civilizing influence at a time when the Carolinas culture was predominantly rural.

The response to economic, social, and cultural conditions in the Carolinas cannot be —

Religion in North Carolina
Top ten denominations by membership

1926

Denomination	Total Members	Percent of All Members
Southern Baptist Convention	385,940	27.4%
Methodist Episcopal Church, South	249,916	17.8%
Negro Baptists	206,807	14.7%
African Methodist Episcopal Zion Church	135,698	9.6%
Presbyterian Church in the United States	77,691	5.5%
Disciples of Christ	38,088	2.7%
Protestant Episcopal Church	33,371	2.4%
Free Will Baptists	31,256	2.2%
Methodist Protestant Church	26,922	1.9%
Methodist Episcopal Church	26,895	1.9%

1990

Denomination	Total Adherents	Percent of All Adherents
Southern Baptist Convention	1,446,228	36.4%
United Methodist Church	605,362	15.2%
Black Baptists (est.)	462,785	11.6%
AME Zion	312,693	7.9%
Presbyterian Church (USA)	205,548	5.2%
Catholic	149,483	3.8%
Evangelical Lutheran Church in America	87,815	2.2%
Episcopal Church	73,664	1.9%
Church of God (Cleveland, TN)	54,828	1.4%
Church of Christ (Disciples of Christ)	50,460	1.3%

Religion in South Carolina
Top ten denominations by membership

1926

Denomination	Total Members	Percent of All Members
Negro Baptists	235,224	26.9%
Southern Baptist Convention	217,104	24.9%
Methodist Episcopal Church, South	135,129	15.5%
African Methodist Episcopal Church	59,372	6.8%
Methodist Episcopal Church	47,749	5.5%
African Methodist Episcopal Zion Church	38,225	4.4%
Presbyterian Church in the United States	37,604	4.3%
United Lutheran Church in America	25,756	2.9%
Protestant Episcopal Church	18,994	2.2%
Roman Catholic Church	9,036	1.0%

1990

Denomination	Total Adherents	Percent of All Adherents
Southern Baptist Convention	894,390	41.4%
Black Baptists (est.)	345,858	16.0%
United Methodist	308,915	14.3%
Presbyterian Church (USA)	93,714	4.3%
Catholic	78,768	3.6%
AME Zion	65,122	3.0%
Evangelical Lutheran Church in America	61,489	2.8%
Episcopal Church	48,655	2.3%
Church of God (Cleveland, TN)	44,422	2.1%
Pentecostal Holiness	25,122	1.2%

should not be — solely a government response. Families under stress, children in need of moorings, communities divided and isolated — all of these, and more, require action by religious congregations, as well as civic groups, businesses, and nonprofit agencies.

There is a kind of tension within many congregations in the Carolinas, as there is across the country. To what extent should a church provide sanctuary, a place where people can get away from the worries of the world for an hour or more on the weekend, where they can pray, refresh themselves, and take care of each other? And to what extent should a church be a community of concern and of action driven by that concern, a place where people work together to feed the hungry, to speak out on issues that have ethical dimensions, and to reach out to transform a secular society?

In addition to a pull-and-tug over how much a church should lean this way or that, two trends also influence the way religion relates to contemporary society in the Carolinas.

Along with population growth and diversity comes religious diversity. In the 1920s, the Carolinas were populated almost exclusively by native-born Protestants. Today, most who declare a religious affiliation still list membership in a Protestant denomination — in fact, Baptists claim a somewhat higher percentage of adherents today than 75 years ago. The larger reality, meanwhile, is that as the Carolinas grow in people, the religious landscape changes. Roman Catholics, Jews, and adherents of Eastern religions have assembled in large enough numbers, especially in the cities and suburbs, that their presence today hardly raises an eyebrow as it would have 20 years ago.

And while it is easy to rank denominations by membership, another facet of the diversity story is that denomination has diminished as a defining characteristic of thousands of Carolinians. Many families move between and among denominations. And today's religious landscape is increasingly marked by the rise of large, nondenominational congregations in our burgeoning suburbs. Young adults, especially including young families with children, have been attracted to such evangelical congregations.

The second trend has to do with church leadership. Within Protestant denominations, women have emerged into the ranks of the clergy, just as they have into business and professions in the wider society. Meanwhile, in an era in which growth in the clergy has not kept pace with population growth, lay leaders have heightened responsibilities in deciding the direction of their congregations.

Some forces are at work that are beyond the control of local churches. The decline of rural communities — brought about by population shifts and vast economic changes — has had an effect on the rural churches that Mr. Duke sought to strengthen. In efforts to maintain and strengthen their viability, churches will surely have to figure out their role in society. What's more, as responsibility for social services is pushed down to the state and local levels, churches will have to come to grips with their duty and potential in seeing to it that rural people get social and medical services.

God's Ballfield
Holly Taylor, 1999
Copyright © 1999 by Holly Taylor

Racial reconciliation amid diversity

Across our two states, Jim Crow is gone, long gone.

For much of this century, most white Carolinians favored keeping racial segregation laws in place. But Jim Crow fell in the face of courageous action by black citizens, including many in the Carolinas.

In the early 1950s, blacks in Summerton, SC, sued the Clarendon County Board of Education, and their action became one of the cases decided in the 1954 Supreme Court ruling that struck down dual school systems. In February 1960, black college students in Greensboro launched the sit-ins that led to the civil rights law opening public accommodations to people of all races.

In Charlotte, a challenge to segregated public schools led to the Supreme Court ruling calling for county-wide busing. Instead of resisting, the city's civic leaders, white and black, rallied to make the landmark ruling work and thus helped lay a basis for its current economic vitality.

Across the region, the elimination of racial segregation laws liberated the economy of the

"Walk to the Supermarket"

An excerpt from *Dreams of Sleep* by Josephine Humphreys

The walk to the supermarket takes her through the black neighborhood of midtown. It is not the way she used to go; she used to detour around the project, sticking to the business streets, or even go to another store. But Iris walks through the project every day. Alice asked, "Isn't it dangerous?" Iris said, "I don't know. I guess it could be, if you're afraid. I'm not because it's just something I've always done. I mean, if you live in it you aren't scared of it."

So Alice started walking Iris's way. The first time she was frightened, as out of place as a clown in her white-woman's clothes and her white skin. People stared at her from windows and porches, from cars. Of course they'd stare. It is unheard of in any Southern city for a white person to walk through one of these places, the old colored towns now gulped into the city and lost behind stores and hotels. The only whites that do it are insurance agents. She has seen them, young twenty-five-year-old men in cheap suits stopping at every house to collect a weekly premium. But this is not the worst of the city, it isn't Bayside, where old people don't leave their houses for months at a time, so frightened are they of what is on the street. No, this is just old colored town. The houses are painted wood, with patches of garden out front. Children hang from the porch railings and old men gather on the comers or in the yard that has a

Carolinas to attract new investment even as it gave African-Americans wider opportunities in education, in the economy, and in political participation.

In matters racial, today's North Carolina and South Carolina stand in stark contrast to the 1920s. Actions by the federal government — the courts, the Congress, and the presidency — brought about change, but it also took action by state and local leaders to manage the transition and make progress.

Today's Carolinas feature a less divided — and divisive — society than 75 years ago. Even

Neighborhood Watch
Mary Edith Alexander, Winter, 1998
Oil on linen
12" x 16"

cable spool set up as a card table, surrounded by busted dinette chairs and Coke crates. There's always a game. Sometimes it is an animated game, the men laugh and toss cards or coins out onto the table, and sometimes it's sedate, a dreamy slow afternoon game under the pecan tree, so quiet the squirrels come down and creep up to within inches of the chairs, getting what nuts have been rejected or overlooked by the children.

It is a pocket of slow, warm living in the middle of town, like a world coexistent with the rest but not visible from it, not from the main traffic arteries or places white people go. Sometimes, if you're lucky, Alice thinks, you can find this: a haven where you least expect it.

───

She no longer feels out of place on this walk, now that she's done it three or four times. Some of the people are always there when she passes, some of the old ones, anyway, who stay near home. One is a woman she sees every time, a large-boned, deep-black woman sweeping her porch or her steps or the sidewalk, even the dirt yard, sweeping every time Alice walks by. The woman is near sixty and shy; her smile is the slow, embarrassed smile of a ten-year-old. Her hair stands away from her head, stiff and shiny. She raises her eyes from the broom toward Alice but

continued...

THE STATE OF THE CAROLINAS

though there is more harmony, our states remain vulnerable to racial frictions and even hostility. Today, the issue of race is different — and yet to some extent the same. Government-imposed and -licensed discrimination is gone, but reconciliation between whites and blacks is not fully completed. Residual economic issues linger, and stereotyping remains prevalent. While the Carolinas face the task of continuing black/white dialogue and reconciliation, our states also have the challenge of managing the transition to a more ethnically diverse society.

The railroad track that separated the white side and the black side of town isn't the defining division that it once was in the Carolinas. For one thing, the settling of Latinos and Asians in our states is restructuring the populations of numerous towns and cities. The changing complexion of the Carolinas has the potential not only to enrich the culture, but also to heighten tensions, especially when the economy cools off and the job market contracts.

What's more, society suffers from a fracturing and a fragmentation, as people huddle together in cultural enclaves, harboring suspicions, biases, and stereotypical notions of each other. Most

---

does not look right at her. They will never speak, too shy of each other, but every day the woman's motions are the same when Alice comes by — the broom stops, the woman's face lifts. Alice takes it as a greeting.

What will happen to all these black people, now the movement is dead, their heroes tucked away in public offices? Was the whole civil rights movement nothing but a minor disturbance in the succession of years? White people have started telling jokes again. Blacks and whites live farther apart than ever, like the double curve of a hyperbolic function, two human worlds of identical misery and passion but occupying opposite quadrants, non-intersecting. In a way, equal but separate. One day something will blow up, but Alice doesn't know whether it will be the world or the South or the Reese family.

Her father, editor of the evening paper for twenty-six years, did not believe in progress, and he was in a position to judge, doing daily business with world events on a scale that ran from fillers to headlines. All of Alice's schooling suggested the world was improving. "Trace the steady growth," the tests said, "in the rights of Americans, from the Declaration of Independence and the Bill of Rights through the subsequent Amendments and the current Civil Rights Movement." But her father said the world was not improving: what looks like progress is only change, he said. Without telling him, she held on to her own girlish trust in a trend for the better, certain, for example, that by the time

Carolinians live in suburbs, not the old close-knit, even if racially divided, communities. Now, a two-earner lifestyle wears families out, and people sit in front of TVs or computers linked to the world but isolated from the neighbor next door.

In such a society, the issue is no longer simply the repealing of laws that granted economic and social privileges to one race. William F. Winter, the chairman of MDC's board and the former governor of Mississippi who served on the Presidential Advisory Board on Race, recently spoke to the "new realities" of race and ethnicity in the South. He declared that our future depends upon avoiding "a stratification of our citizenry" and an understanding of "our mutual interdependence."

"There must be a recognition that the ultimate challenge lies in the educational and economic advancement of people who have gotten left behind," Winter said. "We must get the message out to every household, and especially every poor household, that the only road out of poverty runs by the schoolhouse. Discrimination is not limited to race. The line that separates the well educated from the poorly educated is the harshest fault line of all."

---

she grew up there would be no more maids. People like Estelle would all get master's degrees in counseling, their children would go to medical school.

He has not won yet. She is still not sure about progress. Evidence seems to support him — these houses with sagging porches, the woman sweeping, the old men under the trees — but it's hard to say for sure what such things mean. She does know that the man who doubted progress now sits in front of his television day and night, a self-fulfilled prophecy. He should have given progress a chance. Should have hoped against hope.

Young, he had hoped. But after coming home from Princeton with a degree in philosophy he went to work at the newspaper, where the kind of hope taught at Princeton dissipated. Why do philosophers in the South so often end as newspapermen, poets as doctors? Maybe they crave what's found in pain and loss: a sense of living among other human beings. They'll give up dreams for it.

She turns the corner onto America Street, where the supermarket rises suddenly up out of its parking lot, the biggest supermarket in the state when it was built fifteen years ago, now outdone in dozens of suburban malls. Its long glassy facade is papered with ads for Tide and Crisco and canned corned beef: civilization.

From Dreams of Sleep
Copyright © 1984 by Josephine Humphreys
Viking
Reprinted by permission of the author

Conclusion: strains and pains of growth

When Mr. Duke launched his power company, he aimed to harness the natural forces of flowing rivers for the benefit of a spread-out population. The Carolinas enter the new millennium with high hopes for a brighter future, but the near-future imposes demanding tests of public will and policy: to nurture the young and educate more people to high levels, to contain sprawl and prevent degradation of the environment, to ensure that the chance for prosperity reaches all people and places, to build a cohesive society amid racial and ethnic diversity.

A scan of demographic, economic, and social trends suggests that a series of issues will test the leadership and citizenry of North Carolina and South Carolina in the first decade of the 2000s:

- With the two states having settled into a suburban style of development, they now confront the consequences in terms of traffic-clogged

---

A Parable: Whose Child is This?

by Doris Betts

One day in wise King Solomon's court guards led in a child and a throng of grumbling citizens. Some claimed to own part of this child but many didn't want even one ear or a finger.

"Whose child is this?" King Solomon asked.

"Not my child!" said one. "It's the wrong color!"

Another said, "No, my child's eyes look different."

Said a third, "My child's grown, this can't be mine."

The king was puzzled, because to him the child kept changing — the skin from dark to light; hair curly or straight; eye color, size and gender. To him the child looked both male and female, aged 5 to 25.

"Not mine!" called a citizen. "My child's gifted and talented!"

"Not mine!" said another, "I'd never dress my child in worn-out clothes!"

One woman wore a chip on her shoulder big as a stick of stovewood. "Too quiet for mine!" she shouted. "My boy has a right to carry a knife! My girl can smoke anyplace she chooses!"

Solomon ordered her to join the others arguing to one side. He called up older citizens, already shaking their gray heads. "Not mine!" they chorused, "because I've finished raising my children and taxes are too high already!"

The king hoped a man in academic robes would claim the child, but the educator said, "No, that's not my child but I do recognize him. Or her. That's a per-pupil. I only study theoretical per-pupils in the abstract."

Next, some merchants said that since 100 percent of good old children in the good old days were thoroughfares, heightened demand on water supplies, and a critical need for safe and sanitary waste disposal.

- With population, power, and prosperity increasingly located in metropolitan areas, the two states have distressed rural people and places that may be left farther behind.
- The future of children is at the center of an array of interrelated developments and trends — a shift in welfare policy, a rise in unwed parenthood, an increase in substance abuse, research showing that critical brain development occurs in the early years. And still, in our states, children have a higher rate of poverty than any other population age-group; and too many families lack health insurance, live in dilapidated housing, and suffer the stresses of domestic violence.
- After many years of determined efforts to site clinics and entice doctors and nurses to the rural Carolinas, geography is no longer an insurmountable barrier to quality health care.

---

perfect students, they'd never hire this modern, imperfect child.

Religious leaders now came forward, in sacred garments, giving ecumenical nods and smiles.

"Oh King, that IS our child," they said, "at least one-seventh is ours. Once a week we'll offer this child spiritual nourishment, but (you understand, Oh King) full-time children would track in mud where we worship."

"Surely," King Solomon said, "you teachers have something to say."

The teachers edged forward; many looked tired. "This child could be my pupil," said one, squinting. "I teach so many their faces blur."

Others said, "Is this the first-grader who needs glasses? The middle-schooler who plays hooky or sleeps in class? Is her father suing me for low grades? Does his mother have a big chip on her shoulder?"

Everyone said it: "Not my child!"

The social worker was overworking in the child's bad neighborhood; the policeman was busy arresting the child's older siblings; a senator flung the child a government grant; rock singers and slam-dunkers posed for TV and offered to be role models when they found the time.

Then a brawling, unruly mob poured in, yelling, "That's MY child! I'll take him! Give her to me!"

Poverty came shouting ahead of his gang of Ignore, Despair, Crime, Racism, Unemployment, Drugs and Rage. These ruffians grabbed for the child with greedy, dirty hands.

"STOP!" roared the king, and he ordered guards to banish this rabble.

Then, quietly, he called his subjects out of their separate self-interest groups, and ordered each to look carefully at the child.

All stared at this child and grew silent. It was like looking into a mirror at themselves long ago; like looking through a window at tomorrow.

continued…

But disparities rooted in race and poverty remain, and a large share of the power to close the gaps rests in today's consolidated hospitals.

- These days, public schools educate many more — and more diverse — students than ever before. And now they are being called upon to reach higher standards and demonstrate greater accountability — even as they must reach into the inner city and out to the hinterlands with the same quality of education delivered to the suburbs. In an increasingly demanding economy, a high school diploma these days is less a ticket to satisfying work than to further education.

- Even when the public schools are fully reformed, the 21st century economy will

Children's Quilt
Students of the Lucy Daniels Preschool,
Lucy Daniels Center for Early Childhood
Cary, North Carolina

Those with brown faces saw a brown child; blue eyes gazed into blue. Hispanic, Native American, Asian and the freckled-faced Joneses all ran together in the child's face.

Grandparents foresaw a grown-up child who would fix their cars, treat their cancers. Merchants saw future workers and customers. Politicians looked beyond new voters and widened their vision to see all of North Carolina, all of America.

One-at-a-time, people began pulling up chairs; they said to the teachers: "Here, you sit down! You can't do this educating by yourself! That's not your child, not even my child; it's OUR child."

Together they began planning to give this child schools, books, computers, to provide music and art, to teach the child to think and dance, to write poems, to make just laws.

They were so busy they hardly noticed when wise King Solomon left.

He didn't mind. He was tired. Sometimes the hardest job any ruler has is just to help people find again how wise they are at heart.

"A Parable: Whose Child is This?" by Doris Betts
For the Fourth Inauguration of Governor James B. Hunt, Jr.
Copyright © 1997 by Doris Betts
The News & Observer, January 14, 1997
Reprinted by permission of the author

require more — that is, two or more years of education beyond high school. Both North Carolina and South Carolina face a daunting challenge not only in coping with anticipated enrollment growth in universities and community colleges but also in ensuring that their institutions of higher education respond to the economy's demand and society's need for a more broadly educated workforce and citizenry.

- As the region diversifies ethnically, North Carolina and South Carolina will find their human relations agenda defined by both the past and the future. Even as the states continue to work out white/black disparities lingering from the era of racial segregation and strive to remove educational, employment, and income differences, they must also turn attention to melding new entrants into the mainstream economy and democracy. The issues that surround race have evolved from what they were a generation ago; they have become more textured, multidimensional, and require new language and new approaches.
- Because elected officials serve for short terms and necessarily are drawn to the issues of the moment, slow-developing trends and long-term needs often get short shrift. In the 1920s, James Buchanan Duke understood that, while governments had a role to play in the pursuit of excellence and happiness, a philanthropic initiative could make a large difference by investing in the intellectual infrastructure that we know as universities and delivering health care inside hospital walls. From philanthropy and the nonprofit sector these days, North Carolina and South Carolina need agenda-setting and the connecting of new learning to real-world problems. Without philanthropy insisting on and helping to shape a long-term view, our states may not look beyond the horizon.

Clear evidence, from our own states, points to civic, business, and political leadership as crucial to community health and progress. To continue flourishing, the Carolinas will need a rejuvenation of civic life and the sustained development of creative leadership. The quality of leadership determines the destiny of towns, cities, and even states — especially so in the sphere of race and ethnic relations.

The task ahead for that leadership was elegantly summarized by David Shi, the president of Furman University, in a roundtable discussion

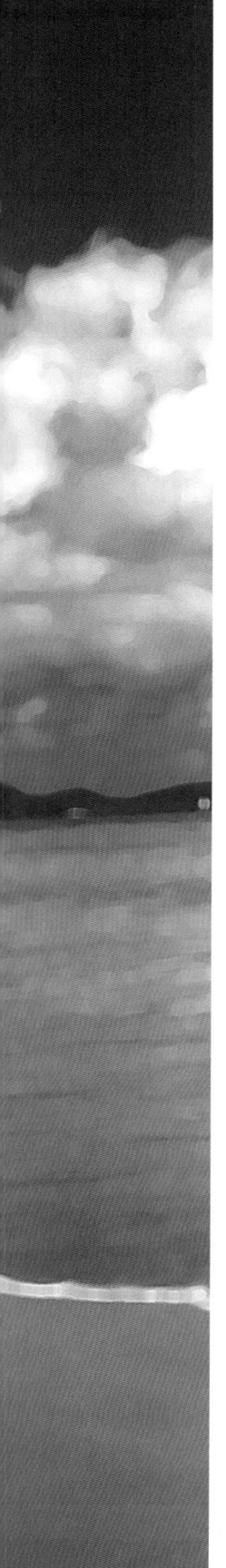

organized for this project. In the 1920s, said Shi, both Carolinas "found themselves struggling to manage survival." Now, after 75 years of advancement in health, education, and economic well-being, North Carolina and South Carolina have reached the point of having the "opportunity to distribute success" and to leave no one out.

Chapter IV
The Carolinas Tomorrow

When James Buchanan Duke established The Endowment, he drew on his own life experiences. He knew, of course, the kinds of philanthropy that other wealthy men of his era had set up, and as a businessman he surrounded himself with technical experts. But in the end, he listened to his own mind and heart in determining how his endowment would go about improving the social and economic prospects of the people of the Carolinas.

How would Mr. Duke, were he alive today, respond to the condition of North Carolina and South Carolina at the end of the 20th century? Undoubtedly, he would again draw on his personal experiences and convictions, blending both quantitative and qualitative information.

This work, too, is a blending — of history and poetry, of art and data. It represents an effort to balance quantitative analysis with expressions

of the heart. To expand our exploration of the state of the Carolinas, this chapter pulls together the thoughts and observations of several well-informed observers of the two states — writers, thinkers, leaders who regularly talk to other well-informed people — whom we asked to ponder these questions:

What are the critical issues facing the Carolinas over the next 25 years, and what is philanthropy's role in addressing those issues?

MDC hosted a roundtable discussion on April 13, 1999, in Chapel Hill. George Autry served as moderator and led the participants through a five-hour interchange on the issues of education, race, health, families and children, religion, leadership, and philanthropy.

The participants were:

— **Doris Betts**, novelist and professor of English at the University of North Carolina at Chapel Hill;

— **Julius Chambers**, chancellor of North Carolina Central University;

— **Bill Friday**, former president of the University of North Carolina system and executive director of the William R. Kenan, Jr. Charitable Trust;

— **Bill Grigg**, chairman-emeritus of Duke Energy Corporation;

— **Susan King**, former chief executive of Steuben Glass and now leader-in-residence of the Hart Leadership Program at Duke University;

— **Tom Lambeth**, executive director of the Z. Smith Reynolds Foundation; and

— **David Shi**, president of Furman University.

Photo courtesy of The Duke Endowment

From left to right:
Bill Friday, Doris Betts, and Susan King

This chapter consists of excerpts from that roundtable discussion with remarks grouped by subject. The participants, to be sure, addressed the questions from different perspectives and, from time to time, offered divergent views. They illustrated the value of discourse in illuminating issues and clarifying problems, a necessity for developing understanding, for seeking solutions, for building consensus.

While the participants had an outline of MDC's findings, their primary assignment was to articulate what they were hearing and seeing in the two states and, most of all, what they are thinking as they look ahead beyond the year 2000.

Betts: There's been an enormous change in expectations. And I mean that in two ways. One is that the population of the '20s and '30s was really a poor, stoic population. Life was tough. They knew it was going to be tough. And so they bore up with things that people will not now endure. Their expectations have been raised.

The other thing that has changed, I think, is the expectations of who is to solve these problems. I do think there is less feeling that philanthropy and churches are to solve them and much more feeling that taxes and government, despite the South's push against that, is to solve them. The problems are still here, they are still huge, but they are a better class of problems. Instead of lynching, you have other kinds of inequities. Instead of being unable to read and write, you cannot function in a computer-run society. They are the same problems, but they have been raised to a slightly higher level of approach. They have not been solved.

Another issue is urban versus suburban versus rural living. People come into Chatham County because they are not charmed any more by urban living, they want to go where the bluebirds are supposed to be. And that's a new movement. The rural areas are changing into kind of large suburbs with big lots, like five or ten acres, but they're still suburbs.

Lambeth: You can still go down to Drummond Point in Eastern North Carolina and see the spot at where the letter was written on shipboard — the first letter written in the English language in the New World — in which an explorer described what he was looking at as "the goodliest land

under the cope of heaven." We have always hoped to live up to that description of North Carolina, and I would hate to see the day come when we couldn't go down there and look out over the water and see that spot, because we won't be goodly any more.

▶ **Grigg**: One of the things that's happening is the internationalization of business. And the other thing that's happening is consolidation of businesses. You see it in banks, you see it in health care with hospitals merging and consolidating. You see it in the energy business. You don't have electric companies and gas companies separate any more, you have energy companies.

So I think that trend toward consolidation, convergence, is going to continue.

▶ **King**: We really have to relook at the whole way in which society is organized, given the information haves and have-nots. It has been quite clear that business couldn't be expected to deliver social services or to take responsibility in this area, and that government was excellent at managing policy, but was lousy at service delivery.

The role of the not-for-profit sector in the delivery of social programs and helping frame the means to those ends is incredibly more important today as we move forward.

▶ **Friday**: We have to redefine what we mean by public service. What is our duty here, not our option, as citizens? It takes leadership, in the best sense of that word, to make progress happen.

Education

The conversation turned specifically to education. The people of the Carolinas today have far different educational needs than those 75 years ago. The South has caught up with the nation in high school graduation, but the economy and the culture are demanding even more education. With few exceptions, people who do not pursue education beyond high school fall behind those who go on to community college or a university in benefiting from the vast economic expansion that has characterized our region at the close of the 20th century. Autry pointed to the advances made by women in education and the economy. But men are lagging behind women in pursuing higher education, and black men are lagging behind white men. A special challenge for the Carolinas is to address the difference in education of white and minority males.

Education Disparities Remain
Educational attainment of population 25 years and older by race and ethnicity — NC and SC*, 1997

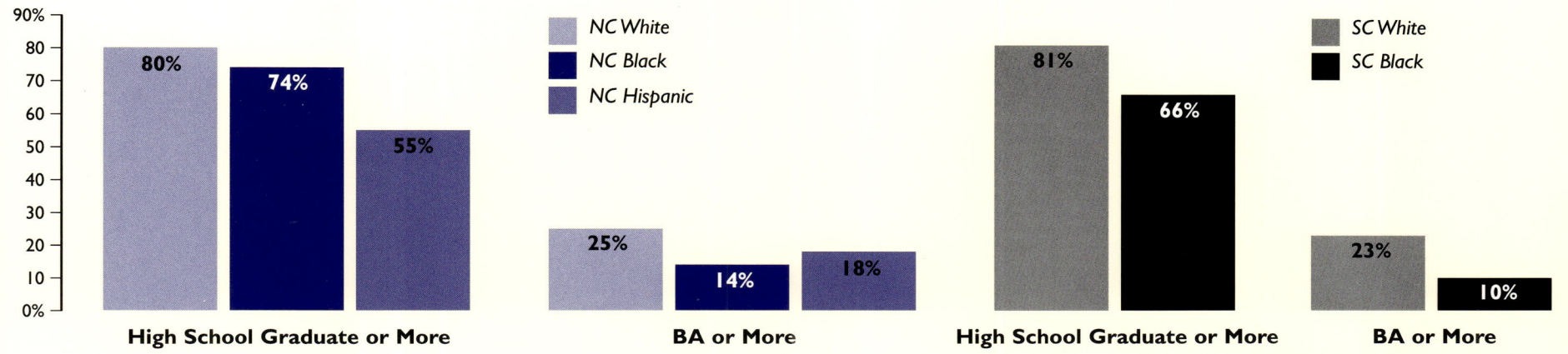

* Data not available for SC's Hispanic population
Source: Statistical Abstract of the United States, 1998

Chambers: We sit here today, and we watch increasing gaps in college-going rates between minorities and whites. We watch increasing gaps between minorities and whites in performances on standardized exams. We watch increasing gaps in job opportunities for minorities and nonminorities. Those are areas where I think we can do something.

I think we all should look at what happens when we grant, for example, affirmative action to make sure that people get a chance to get an education. Whether it's going to be an education at Chapel Hill or an education at Central, giving people the opportunity to really learn something is crucial and helps to build a better society for all of us.

Grigg: You come out of school today, and when you get that diploma, you're educated. A year from now you're behind because of the things that are changing.

So I think that business is going to have to be in the business of education. And that colleges and universities are going to have to be in the business of continuing education. I think adult education is increasingly important.

▶ **Betts:** The schools in Chatham County, where I live, were absolutely unprepared for the influx of the Hispanic population. Siler City is not a rich town, and now almost one-fourth of its children are Hispanic, many of them speaking little or no English. And you have teachers who haven't been prepared to be bilingual.

So you've got to trace that all the way back to the schools of education. And we're way behind, we're way behind. And that's a new form of illiteracy if English is a strange language to you.

▶ **Friday:** It's so interesting to hear people talk today about what's happened to the teacher in the classroom and how are we going to pull her or him out of this maze of being truant officer or cake salesman and let them really teach. Create a professional; this is the idea.

It's rather significant that a story in this morning's paper said the average major league baseball player this year will make $1,360,000, on average. That's more money than the best teacher in the best high school in Raleigh will make in her entire lifetime. I think it says something about our culture. Society should never take its eye off this issue.

▶ **Lambeth:** Not long ago I was in a school not far beyond where Doris and I grew up and met five teachers who were really extraordinary because of their commitment in this rural school system to try to do something about introducing their children to the arts and other enrichment activities. One of them looked at me and said, "Do you understand how hard it is to work with children who arrive at school already defeated?"

Bill Friday

Photo courtesy of The Duke Endowment

And that's a very powerful message.

I think we know everything we need to know about how to improve public schools. Everything. There is a model everywhere. There is a pilot project. There is nothing else we need to know. What we lack is the will to do it.

A constant challenge and frustration for organized philanthropy is how you create the will to do something. It is true that nothing in this state very important has ever been accomplished without the support of the business community, but it is just as true that if our public schools are going to be what they ought to be — and that means K through graduate school — it is going to be because the public, because they are the public's schools, decides that they will be. I think that we, as funders, have to work hard at being strategic in our role of supporting education.

We are clearly the source of survival for higher education, we're the margin of excellence for public education. Our funding has to be strategic. We are not appropriation committees. We have no business relieving the public of their obligation to decide whether their children are important enough to invest in them. And I think that's a constant challenge to us about our funding.

Abandoned Schoolhouse on Long Branch

from Source by Fred Chappell

The final scholar scrawls his long
Black name in aisle dust, licks the air
With his tendril double tongue,
Coils up in shadow of a busted chair

And dozes like the farmer boys
Who never got straight the capital
Of Idaho, found out the joys
Of long division, or learned what all

Those books were all about. Most panes
Are gone now and the web-milky windows
Are open to the world. Gold dust-grains
Swirl up, and show which way the wind blows.

K.B. + R.J., cut deep
In a darkened heart on the cloakroom wall.
Now Katherine Johnson and Roger sleep
Quite past the summons of the morning bell.

The teacher sleeps narrow too, on yonder
Side of Sterling Mountain, as stern
With her grave as with a loutish blunder
In the Bible verse she set them to learn.

Sunset washes the blackboard. Bees
Return to the rich attic nest
Where much is stored. Their vocalese
Entrances the native tranquil dust.

"Abandoned Schoolhouse on Long Branch" by Fred Chappell
From *Source*
Copyright © 1985 by Fred Chappell
Louisiana State Press
Reprinted by permission of the author

▸ **Friday:** In writing about the Southern states recently, *Education Week* said about North Carolina, "It's a fit-and-start place." We get into a fit about something, we start it and never finish solving the problem. For the last 13 years [as executive director of the William R. Kenan, Jr. Charitable Trust] I've had an opportunity to do something that I didn't in the previous 30 [at the University of North Carolina]. And I've been into soup kitchens, and I've been in literacy classes, and I've been in homeless shelters. What you find is that there's another world out there that the academic community really doesn't know about, doesn't understand.

The Carolinas are fortunate to have highly developed systems of community and technical colleges, as well as research and regional universities. Autry pointed out that universities in North Carolina have more doctoral research programs ranked among the top 20 in their respective fields than any other Southern state. Colleges and universities can be powerful architects of our future, and the panelists were asked to reflect on what we should expect of higher education in responding to social and economic issues and in developing leadership.

▸ **Shi:** From the point of view of small, private liberal arts colleges, I would say the developments of late include a growing emphasis and maturation of formal leadership development programs.

Most of the private colleges in the Carolinas have explicit, structured leadership development

Lead thou me to the rock that is higher than I
Donald Furst
Mixed intaglio
14.25" x 9.75"

programs intended to stimulate, nurture, and apply the leadership potential of our students.

Related to this development is the continuing evolution of service learning. What has happened in the last 15 years is a growing intersection of the academic program with social service activity, so that more and more courses are incorporating social change, social involvement into their academic curriculum. It gives much greater depth to that social activism, that social involvement, on the part of the students.

The third, and still-related, activity is an emphasis on engaged learning on the part of our students. That is, more and more of our colleges, and, more and more of our professors, are now insisting that students not just be passive recipients of information and knowledge, but that they be active participants and even collaborators in the classroom, in the laboratory, and, perhaps most imaginatively, outside of the classroom and off the campus in the form of internships, undergraduate research opportunities, experiential learning.

An old Chinese proverb says, "Tell me and I will forget; show me and I will remember; involve me and I will understand." And I think that's really what's driving this nationwide emphasis on more active forms of learning.

David Shi

Photo courtesy of The Duke Endowment

▶ **Friday**: Duke University's program in ethics among young people illustrates a point I think we want to be careful about when we talk about leadership. They're not talking about management skills. They're talking about moral issues and character development and integrity questions.

You can't solve societal problems now if the universities don't reach out. I think we should quit saying it's an option. It's a duty.

What I am so anxious to see is somebody step

forward in the political arena and say, "We're going to do these things." Let's stop talking. We know a lot about what we need to do. Let's just get up the nerve. Maybe you don't serve but one term. So be it. If we don't, I don't think we're fulfilling the trust that was put in our hands, our generation.

Race

The conversation moved on to race, which Autry described as "our oldest, thorniest, trickiest, most explosive problem" in North Carolina and South Carolina. Race, as a problem, has changed. It has evolved. It isn't getting any easier. It's gotten more complex. The Carolinas, as well as the nation, are now a multiracial, multiethnic society. Tom Lambeth began by recalling a survey on racial attitudes in North Carolina commissioned by the Z. Smith Reynolds Foundation.

Lambeth: The statistic that always nagged at me from that survey was that we found that the point of greatest communication between the races in North Carolina was shopping malls. Not exactly a great kind of communication. We talked about churches, we talked about schools, we talked about civic organizations. We talked about everything. The one place that races in North Carolina agreed that they had the most contact with other races was shopping malls. Sort of a sad fact, it seems to me.

One thing that has changed — clearly a positive — is that we are reacting more to projects that come to us out of the African-American and the Latino communities, not that come from predominantly white institutions or organizations that are trying to reach out, although there's some of that.

In our case certainly and in the case of most organized philanthropy in this state, the funders look more like the whole state. Not just like it, but boards are more representative by race and by gender.

The arguments have gone on in Winston-Salem about whether it matters that the school board has women on it or has African-Americans on it. And there are always these extremely well-meaning white males that say, "I'm interested in everybody" and really mean it. And what they have to understand is the same questions don't get

> *And what [white males] have to understand is the same questions don't get asked if everybody around the table is the same. Whatever their good intentions are, there are questions that get asked when people of a different gender are present. There are questions that get asked when people who are of a different race are present.*

78   THE CAROLINAS

asked if everybody around the table is the same. Whatever their good intentions are, there are questions that get asked when people of a different gender are present. There are questions that get asked when people who are of a different race are present. There are questions that get asked when people of different ages are represented. It doesn't necessarily reflect the lack of good intentions and commitment on the part of anybody present, it's just that the questions don't get asked and answers aren't required if everybody is alike.

▶ **Chambers:** The race issue isn't just whites discriminating against blacks today. It's everybody discriminating against anyone who is different.

In Durham today, or Raleigh, or Charlotte, the communication gap is terrible. And it would help, I think, if foundations would fund efforts to promote more dialogue among people.

I don't think you're going to really bridge this gap or begin to address this issue of race effectively until you can figure out ways to really bring people together. And you're going to have to encourage black people and white people and Hispanics and Asians, all, to sit down at a table together and to get their kids in school together and to get the parents working together.

Another problem is that there are barriers that I don't think we are ready to focus on. Why, for example, do we have black kids scoring 100 points less on an SAT than white kids? I don't think anybody can prove that they are just mentally inferior. I think it's a problem with experiences and a problem with what they have, the kind of experiences they have at home, the kind of parental guidance that they have.

Tom Lambeth

Photo courtesy of The Duke Endowment

Technicolor™ States
Population by race/ethnicity, 1997

	Total	White	Black	American Indian, Eskimo, Aleut	Asian, Pacific Islander	Hispanic Origin (any race)
North Carolina	7,425,000	5,466,000 (73.6%)	1,643,000 (21.9%)	95,000 (1.3%)	92,000 (1.2%)	149,000 (2.0%)
South Carolina	3,760,000	2,549,000 (67.8%)	1,124,000 (29.9%)	9,000 (0.2%)	32,000 (0.9%)	46,000 (1.2%)
United States	267,636,000	194,571,000 (72.7%)	31,363,000 (11.7%)	2,322,000 (0.9%)	10,033,00 (3.7%)	29,347.000 (11.0%)

Source: U.S. Census Bureau Estimates

How much money does it take to teach a kid who grows up in a poor home? And how do you get away with saying, "I give an equal dollar for students" when one student may need ten dollars in order to build a bridge. We won't face that issue. And when we don't, I think we get racial groups standing back criticizing everything.

▶ **Grigg:** It all comes down to leadership, doesn't it? You've got to have somebody out front saying, "This is the way it's going to be." I think in my own company of a great example of that. Back in the 1970s, we began to integrate our construction force for the first time. Then in the end of the '70s demand fell off, so we were canceling some projects and had to lay people off.

The question was, whom do you lay off? The time-honored tradition was that you lay off the junior people. Well, if we did that, we would have laid off the minorities. And Bill Lee, to his everlasting credit, said, "We're not going to do that." And we worked out a more equitable system.

The aftermath of that decision set a whole new tone for that company. One man at the top saying, "This is the way it's going to be; this is the right thing to do." And it makes all the difference in the world.

▶ **Chambers:** If black people, or some of them, say they would rather return to a black school and white people say they would rather return to a white school, then somebody, some leader, has to say, "We can't have that kind of reverse discrimination." Otherwise, I think you're going to have resegregation.

Shi: In addition to the obvious improvements in terms of statutory or legal rights over the last 75 years, probably the most important but less visible improvement is the emergence of a black middle- and upper-middle- and professional class of leaders.

And that's probably the single most important factor at work in Greenville in helping to develop and sustain programs directed at poverty, educational inequality, criminal justice inequalities, as well as the familial dynamics that are all interrelated.

King: Hope is what the poor don't have; hope is what the young black male does not have. And we can focus on how do we encourage and enrich the sense of community that involves everybody in the same community instead of these little disparate enclaves as everybody sort of self-segregates.

Chambers: What bothers me is that most of us today close our eyes to the fact that there are problems. I think historically we looked at things and thought about fault, "Who caused this?"

Photo courtesy of The Duke Endowment

Susan King

Race is still a pervasive issue. And in the minority community people are quite disturbed that people don't seem to want to address it.

I don't think I overstate the case in saying hardly anybody wants to address poverty. I think we recognize it's there, we recognize all the disparities reflected in the statistics. And yet we leave them there. I don't see that real commitment to addressing it at the present time.

Shi: In Greenville right now, a biracial task force is wrestling with issues of criminal justice. And that is a very thorny thicket because statistics are difficult to come by, they're controversial to interpret, and the criminal justice system is very difficult to reform.

So, I think, that probably is going to be the continuing focal point of racial issues, the equitable treatment of citizens in the criminal justice system.

Health

Autry opened the discussion on health care by observing that Mr. Duke and The Endowment helped give North Carolina one of the best and strongest nonprofit health-care systems in the country. But he also observed that both states have not achieved adequate health among the poor and among African-Americans. How, he asked, can we make hospitals pay attention to what goes on outside their walls as well as to the quality of care within their walls? In an era of "bigness" — big hospitals, big HMOs, big insurance, big doctors' practices — how can we provide more adequate health care for those who now have limited access to quality and affordable care?

 **Betts**: I think about prevention as the primary development coming out of our medical centers. There's much more emphasis, I think, on exercising and prevention and better diet.

But I do know too many people have no health insurance whatsoever and can be wiped out overnight. And they are not always in what we might call the underclass. There are plenty of people making what I used to consider a passable wage who may or may not have health insurance because of peculiarities of different kinds of jobs.

So I think the problem of guaranteeing care for people is increasingly difficult. Among the

---

"On Nurses"

An excerpt from *A Whole New Life* by Reynolds Price

I recall clearly though that all those days and wakeful nights were the summit of pain in my life till now. The one good memory of that whole stay in Duke Hospital was the constant kindness I received from nurses. From all my stays I recall no nurse — woman or man — who was less than helpful. My strongest memories though, and thanks, are for the calm black women who'd answer my calls in the predawn hours of this painful stay, when I needed help to turn in bed.

By something more than an accidental grace, more than most others, those women were able to blend their professional code with the oldest natural code of all — mere human connection, the simple looks and words that award a suffering creature his or her dignity. Not at all incidentally, they were the only persons in my recollection of my hospital stays who ever asked my opinion of my care — was I being treated well? What else did I need? Certainly no medical doctor ever asked. Many times since, I've thought that if I were ever to donate a work of art to Duke, I'd commission a realistic bronze statue of a black woman in a nurse's uniform and ask that it stand by the hospital door.

From *A Whole New Life*
Copyright © 1982, 1986, 1990, 1994 by Reynolds Price
Plume/Penguin
Reprinted by permission of the author

trends to pay attention to is the growing impersonality that we all fear.

Since I've worked with my mother's situation at age 87, I have never seen so much ludicrous paperwork that the elderly are asked to do, which I puzzled over for hours. If you are on Medicare or Medicaid, you really need to be a genius simply to fill out the forms. Or, if you're on one of those prescription systems and you call long distance and they say, "Now, punch '3.' Now, give us your backwards Social Security number and punch '5.' " It's just dreadful.

So there's an inhumanity at a place where we need to be more humane. It's not just Medicare. It's private insurance, too.

▸ **Grigg**: There's a pilot neighborhood clinic now operating in a Charlotte community in a facility built by a church, furnished by The Endowment, and staffed by the Carolinas Medical Center — a good partnership. It's a wonderful way to provide services for a community that really didn't have medical services before.

And there's a Head Start facility there with 800 kids that they used to have to put into buses and take downtown to get shots. Now they can administer the shots and check the sore throats right there on site.

It's a great example of a partnership involving the hospital and The Endowment and the churches, which incidentally I think are the most underutilized institution in America.

Families and children

The age of orphans and half-orphans, cared for in large institutions, has passed into an age of foster care, proliferating one-parent families, and rising incidence of abuse and neglect. Autry steered the participants into a consideration of several intersecting trends with regard to families and children, poverty, and the quality of family life. How can we bring our institutions — not only government, but also community organizations and nonprofits — to bear in raising the quality of family life in the Carolinas?

▸ **Shi**: At Furman, we've been involved in a collaboration [funded by The Endowment] among the Greenville County Schools, the Greenville Memorial Hospital System, and an array of related agencies. The simplest way to explain it is we have created a reverse magnet school. That is, instead of trying to bring together the most talented kids in a particular discipline or area, we brought together at-risk kids for pre-K through third grade.

The hospital system has created a clinic in the school for both diagnostic, preventive, and inoculation treatment. The school not only provides education for the children, but provides education for the parent or guardian to gain a GED certificate.

Walk down the hallways, and on one side you'll see a classroom of five-year-olds, and on the other side you'll see a classroom of their parents at the same time. And the parents, in turn, help out at recess and lunch.

A group of black leaders in our community is now talking about constructing a community recreation center that would include a medical clinic as well as a police substation. It would have overnight beds for children whose single parent might have been arrested or might have disappeared. For such kids suddenly in transition to institutional foster care, they will have an immediate need for a place to sleep that night.

It is beginning to echo and reverberate, this concept of multiagency, holistic organization, and institutional emphasis on problems that are indeed organically related. That is, family, faith, school, medicine.

▶ **Friday**: I sat there in a little place in Kentucky watching this happen. They put the mother and the children on the same school bus, and they ride in together. First time they've had a warm breakfast together in their lives. Twelve mothers there, each of them had been abandoned by their husbands, all of them are poverty-stricken cases, had children 3, 4, and 5 years of age. They'd never had an hour in their lives where they sat and played together. We worked that in at 10:30 every day. Two meals a day together. And this is togetherness. She was getting a GED, and the child was getting all the prekindergarten and kindergarten training you'd ever want to get.

▶ **Grigg**: Where we really have a serious problem is in the lower preschool and early school. When somebody gets to be a 12th-grader, affirmative action is not going to work if that person is not ready to go into college. We've got to tackle that issue early on.

How do we do for early childhood education what we've done for higher education? How do you solve the problem of a first-grade teacher confronting one child who doesn't know red from yellow from blue and another who already knows how to read?

Friday: Smart Start needs to be in every county. And yet Governor Hunt has literally had to stop doing everything else, concentrate on that one program, get it funded, or that's lost.

Shi: That's being mimicked in South Carolina with a program called First Steps.

Chambers: Dr. Friday has been raising this issue of poverty, and his is really about the only voice I hear crying out there as much as he has about our need to really look at poor people. He's quite right, it's a different world out here. It's a different world right here in Durham and Chapel Hill.

And I don't think many people know that world. And I don't think many black people or white people know that world. Unless we do something to bridge that gap and to make sure that these children get an education and have some hope for the future, we're going to have — I call it — a cancer of the American society.

And, you know, it cuts across everything we do: health care, prenatal care, housing, going to college.

Betts: When Buck Duke was setting things up, he didn't have to think about crack babies.

Friday: There are nearly a million people in North Carolina who don't make more than a poverty wage. That's a sixth of the population. One out of three either does not have health care; or, if he or she has any semblance of health care, a catastrophic illness wipes out the family resources. And a sick child can't learn in school; neither can a battered child.

But who do you hear speaking for this?

Julius Chambers

Photo courtesy of The Duke Endowment

THE CAROLINAS TOMORROW

There are nearly a million people in North Carolina who don't make more than a poverty wage. That's a sixth of the population. One out of three either does not have health care; or, if he or she has any semblance of health care, a catastrophic illness wipes out the family resources. And a sick child can't learn in school; neither can a battered child.

What do you hear anybody saying around the state? Nothing. Now, this is a paralysis that's going to hurt corporate North Carolina more than it's going to hurt anybody else, because these people form part of the workforce.

Now what is the alternative that the Great Old State of North Carolina has put itself into? We're going to stand up over there next week in a committee hearing and hear it said that the only way we can carry out the mandate of the North Carolina Supreme Court for a sound basic education for every child is to institute a lottery.

There is a great need out there for somebody to step forward now in a leadership role, even at the expense of maybe not winning next time, to define this community that's out here that nobody wants to talk about. For the poor, the children, the displaced, the disadvantaged, there is no spokesman now like there used to be.

▶ **Grigg**: Our major problem has to do with the family and the whole range of family issues: early childhood education, breakup of the family, the family unit. I think that this is a problem for business, I think it's a problem for education, I think it's a problem for all of us.

Studies have shown that virtually every child who makes it into college, for example, had an adult role model to look to for advice, to lean on for support. Normally, it's a parent, but it may not always be. It might be a minister, a Scoutmaster, a teacher. But it's a one-on-one kind of a solution.

Which leads me to the conclusion that, although government will continue to play a major role in addressing societal needs, the solution to many of our problems is going to be at the local level. It's going to be one-on-one, eyeball-to-eyeball, you and me, dealing with problems that are unique to us.

…although government will continue to play a major role in addressing societal needs, the solution to many of our problems is going to be at the local level. It's going to be one-on-one, eyeball-to-eyeball, you and me, dealing with problems that are unique to us.

Faith and spiritual life

Autry noted that it is sometimes difficult to involve religious institutions in economic and social action, in part because many churches believe their role is fostering personal salvation. And he also noted that many worshippers want their churches to be a haven of peace and reflection, away from the "cultural bombardment" of the outside world. Shi picked up the conversation by noting a distinct difference between Mr. Duke's era and the temper of our times.

▶ **Shi**: A problem facing religious life and religious institutions has been the growing emphasis on galvanic social issues that tend to fracture not only denominations, but individual congregations.

Whether it be abortion or homophobia or, in our two states most recently, the lottery and video poker, these issues are so superheated that they exacerbate fragmentation rather than facilitate community dialogue. They presume a dogmatic stance on either side of the issue.

▶ **Betts**: There was a time when for a boy to grow up — and it usually was a boy — to be a minister was a very high calling. I've been on the board for a theological seminary. And the ministry is now being entered by a lot of women and a certain number of minority students. But a high percentage are second-career, older people. It's a different kind of ministry, for good or for ill.

It seems to me that when Buck Duke was coming along, one of the big functions of the church was to comfort people who were essentially poor and struggling and having a hard time, and to build character and have them persevere.

Most of our population now is in the middle,

Doris Betts

Photo courtesy of The Duke Endowment

THE CAROLINAS TOMORROW 87

and most of them don't go to church. They have an institutional suspicion. So all the churches are coping with this middle group that they are not getting to come back until they get much older.

▶ **King**: In the spiritual area, attention to establishment of churches, I think, may not be the issue so much as the use of churches as organizing facilities for providing good in the community.

▶ **Grigg**: The local church is becoming more autonomous and what you're seeing is the development of a lay ministry. The role of the minister is changing. The minister is no longer the one you come to when the barn burns down. You no longer look to that person to do everything. The ministry of the church is going to be carried out by laypeople.

And if that's true, I think there's a tremendous opportunity there. I think probably our greatest wasted resource is our churches. The wealth that's there, the talent that's there, the facilities that are there offer tremendous opportunity to do good things addressing all these problems that we're talking about.

Technology and quality of life

Mr. Duke used technology — in his case, electricity generated from water power — both to improve the economic prospects of Carolinians and to make his philanthropy possible. How might the technologies of the Information Age be used to allow Carolinians a higher quality of life with increased opportunity?

▶ **Shi**: There's no doubt that the Information Age, in theory, gives us the potential to redistribute population and transform the very nature of the workplace. The problem at the moment, and certainly in the near future, is ensuring access both to the education necessary to take advantage of the Information Age and to the hardware and software.

It's one thing to talk about it in theory. It's another to realize that many of our public schools are a generation or two generations behind in terms of the equipment, the software, and the teacher training.

And then we've got the problem of so many disadvantaged students and families not having a computer at home, and yet more and more teachers and professors are presuming that their students have computers at home and have ready

Bill Grigg

access to computers. Otherwise, the computer technology becomes, ironically, an instrument that widens the gap between rich and poor, advantaged and disadvantaged.

▶ **Lambeth**: There's a program called ExplorNet in which high school kids are taught how to repair computers. Simultaneously, they learn how to operate computers. And they are doing this for their school system. In Johnston County recently, for example, they reduced the cost of putting computers in their classrooms by $100,000; they taught a large number of their rural students how to repair computers and, therefore, gave them a skill that is highly marketable — across all sorts of economic and social and racial lines — while teaching them how to be computer literate.

▶ **Grigg**: We have moved away from agriculture and textiles. High tech, in particular, is going to offer tremendous opportunity. I think the Information Age is really a great thing for the Carolinas.

But businesses are going to get bigger, are going to consolidate. And with that comes less personalization. Business is going to be more impersonal, and it's going to create problems. Anxiety goes up in that kind of environment.

▶ **Shi**: The U.S. Chamber of Commerce last year published a white paper looking at the future of information technology. It stressed that there's currently a shortage of 250,000 information technology professionals in the United States. In the face of that shortfall, which they predict is only going to increase with time, last year all colleges and universities produced a total of 25,000 computer science majors.

This shortfall affords the Carolinas a strategic

opportunity. The technical colleges today are doing an adequate job of entry-level IT training, but they're not turning out systems analysts, project managers.

That's the critical node within the IT sector: people who not only have the technical skills, but more importantly, have business acumen and interpersonal skills so that they can be both visionary and effective managers within their segment of a corporate activity.

Our challenge at the moment is to mobilize corporate and governmental support to help South Carolina catch up in creating the infrastructure for such IT development.

We're in conversation with a small group of people about creating something like Research Triangle Park, but with a unique centerpiece. Instead of following the RTP model of creating a Research Triangle Institute as its hub, we're talking about a technology research park whose hub would be a Center for Information Technology Education.

▶ **Lambeth:** When it gets to technology, we might actually be developing an interest in looking at the implications of distance learning to higher education. While everybody seems to have enthusiasm for that, we have some concern about what that means to these traditional centers of scholarship.

It seems to me that one of the things we ought to be concerned about in public policy over the next several years is the response of the public system, because it has an implication to the private institutions also, to this growth in enrollment.

Because, while it's real and it's got to be dealt with, I am frightened at the thought of quick fixes to deal with it.

▶ **Betts:** How to benefit from technology without being overwhelmed by it — I think that's going to continue to be a real question.

If Mr. Duke were with us today...

At the conclusion of the panel discussion, Autry asked the participants to talk about what they would tell Mr. Duke were he here among us these days. The question was posed as a way to have the panelists explore two broad topics: What are the most critical issues facing the Carolinas over the next 25 years, and how might philanthropy address these issues?

▶ **Grigg**: There's a tremendous opportunity for foundations. I think foundations can experiment in ways that government can't. Foundations can innovate. Foundations can serve as conveners.

Foundations occupy a unique position. They are viewed as impartial, they don't have an ax to grind. And they are, I think, uniquely positioned to convene various elements of the community to deal with problems, and to experiment, to find solutions in ways that government simply can't.

▶ **King**: Look beyond traditional arrangements, be willing to take some risks, and don't be afraid to fail.

Bring hospital boards together. It would be very interesting if you were to have an annual conference — maybe you could do it regionally because there's so many — and invite all of the members of the public hospital boards and do some presentations about trends and what is happening long-term. They have a big influence in their communities and on their hospitals.

▶ **Shi**: I'm excited about the opportunities afforded by the new emphasis of The Endowment on multiagency community initiatives through the Children and Families program and hope that we can sustain those innovations perennially rather than it just being a two-year or a three-year effort, and then we move on to something else.

▶ **Lambeth**: Race and poverty are still the great issues, and education is the strategy for dealing with them. I would tell him that the nonprofit community needs to be as entrepreneurial as the for-profit community.

If you really want your philanthropy to be relevant, it is important to structure opportunities to know about the world in which you are making grants.

I would say to Mr. Duke,

> *Foundations occupy a unique position. They are viewed as impartial, they don't have an ax to grind. And they are, I think, uniquely positioned to convene various elements of the community to deal with problems, and to experiment, to find solutions in ways that government simply can't.*

THE CAROLINAS TOMORROW

listen to all these wise people, get the best information you can, and then, if you think it best, ignore us all, and do what you think is right. That is what philanthropy is all about.

▶ **Grigg**: Philanthropy is not a tool, a toy, of the Dukes and the Reynolds and the Rockefellers anymore. Philanthropy is available to everybody, and it's growing.

Of the $130 billion that was given to charity last year, over half of it was given by people who make less than $50,000 a year. In fact, community foundations are growing faster than any other charitable vehicle.

But this also creates an opportunity and a challenge for the more established foundations, like Duke and like Reynolds, because they need to exercise a leadership role in helping these other foundations, these smaller foundations, be accountable, help them develop their strategies, the way they operate, the way they communicate, the way they report, the way they are managed.

I think collaboration among foundations is going to be increasingly important. I think it's a tremendous opportunity.

▶ **Shi**: If we were to have the luxury of talking to Mr. Duke at this stage, it seems to me that one of the major changes over these 75 years is that, whereas in the 1920s both Carolinas found themselves struggling to manage survival, we now find ourselves with the opportunity to distribute success to more people across our two states.

Roundtable Participants

Doris Betts

Betts is Alumni Distinguished Professor of English at the University of North Carolina at Chapel Hill, where she teaches creative writing. A native of Statesville, North Carolina, she is the author of eight novels and short-story collections.

Julius Chambers

A native of a small rural community east of Charlotte, North Carolina, Chambers is Chancellor of North Carolina Central University in Durham. A former litigator, Chambers successfully argued several landmark civil rights cases before the United States Supreme Court and was Director-Counsel of the NAACP Legal Defense and Educational Fund in New York City.

William C. Friday

Friday is President-Emeritus of the University of North Carolina, and he now serves as Executive Director of the William R. Kenan, Jr. Charitable Trust in Chapel Hill, North Carolina. Included in his numerous honorary degrees and awards are the National Humanities Medal in 1997 and the World Citizen Award in 1996.

William H. Grigg

Grigg, who grew up in Albemarle, North Carolina, is Chairman-Emeritus and former Chief Executive Officer of Duke Energy Corporation in Charlotte, North Carolina. In addition to serving on several corporate and civic boards, he is Chairman of the Board of the Foundation for the Carolinas.

Susan King

King is Leader-in-Residence of the Hart Leadership Program at the Sanford Institute of Public Policy, Duke University. She is also a member of the Duke University Board of Trustees, the Coca-Cola Board of Directors, the National Public Radio Board of Trustees, and the MDC Board of Directors.

Tom Lambeth

Lambeth, a native of Clayton, North Carolina, is Executive Director of the Z. Smith Reynolds Foundation in Winston-Salem, North Carolina. He has served as chairman of the Board of Trustees of the University of North Carolina at Chapel Hill and was the first chairman of the North Carolina Teaching Fellows Commission.

David Shi

A prominent historian and the author of several books, Shi is President of Furman University in Greenville, South Carolina. Formerly, he was Frontis W. Johnston Professor of History at Davidson College, where he also served as the history department chairman from 1987 to 1992.

Photo courtesy of Duke Power Archives

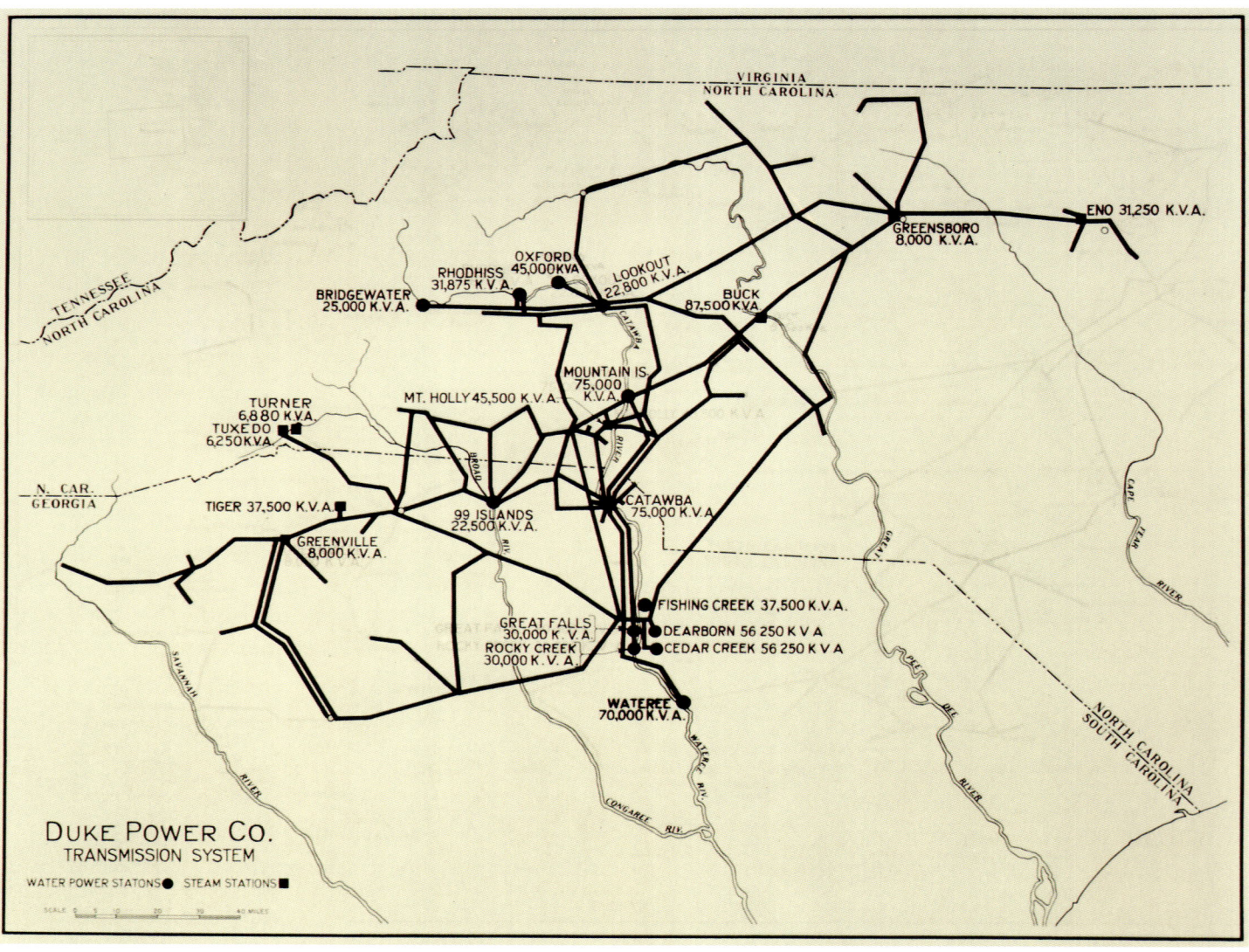

1927 Duke Power Company transmission system map.

Literary Contributors

James Applewhite

Applewhite is a professor of English at Duke University. He has published seven books of poetry and critical essays on modern American poetry, Southern literature, and modernist and postmodernist aesthetics in poetry and visual art.

Doris Betts

Betts is Alumni Distinguished Professor of English at the University of North Carolina at Chapel Hill, where she teaches creative writing. A native of Statesville, North Carolina, she is the author of eight novels and short-story collections.

Walter Buchanan

Buchanan, who is deceased, earned a Master of Science degree from Ohio State University in 1929. Buchanan served as Assistant Supervisor of Vocational Agricultural Teachers in Negro Schools of South Carolina and Dean of the School of Agriculture at South Carolina State College. Artist Beverly Buchanan is his daughter.

Fred Chappell

A native of Canton, North Carolina, Chappell is the Poet Laureate of North Carolina and the author of six novels, two books of short stories, 13 volumes of poetry, a book of essays, and an anthology. He also finds time to teach at the University of North Carolina at Greensboro.

Michael Chitwood

Chitwood, born and raised in the foothills of the Virginia Blue Ridge, now is a freelance writer living in Chapel Hill, North Carolina. He has published three books of poetry, including *The Weave Room*, and an essay collection, *Hitting Below the Bible Belt*. Chitwood is also a regular commentator for WUNC-FM public radio.

Pat Conroy

Conroy is a resident of the Lowcountry of South Carolina, which figures prominently in both his nonfiction and fiction. He is the author of five best-selling books, all of which have been made into motion pictures, and numerous articles and essays, including the Foreword to Jonathan Green's *Gullah Images*.

Josephine Humphreys

Humphreys is a native of Charleston, South Carolina, where she returned after studying at Duke University and Yale University. The first of her three novels, *Dreams of Sleep*, won the PEN/Faulkner Award. She also has written many articles and is a contributor to several essay collections.

Reynolds Price

A native of Macon, North Carolina, Price is James B. Duke Professor of English at Duke University, where he has taught since 1959. He is the author of critically acclaimed novels, short stories, poems, plays, memoirs, and translations from the Bible.

Samuel Proctor

Proctor, who died in 1997, had a distinguished career as a pastor, preacher, college president, and teacher. He served as president of North Carolina A&T University from 1960 to 1964 and taught at Duke University, the University of Wisconsin, Vanderbilt University, Yale University, and Rutgers University. He was the first African-American to deliver a sermon at Duke Chapel.

Visual Arts Contributors

Mary Edith Alexander

Alexander, now a resident of Charlotte, was raised in North Carolina. A Merit Scholar and masters graduate of Cranbrook Academy of Art, she is a recent recipient of a regional artist project grant from the Mecklenburg Arts and Science Council. Her work has been the subject of solo and group exhibitions across the United States.

Tarleton Blackwell

A native of Manning, South Carolina, Blackwell was the Duncanson Artist-in-Residence at the Taft Museum of Art and was the recipient of a Southern Arts Federation/National Endowment for the Arts Regional Fellowship in Painting, Drawing, and Works of Paper. Blackwell teaches art in the Manning public schools.

Beverly Buchanan

Buchanan, a native of Fuquay, North Carolina, spent her formative years in Orangeburg, South Carolina, where her father, Walter Buchanan, was dean of the School of Agriculture at South Carolina State College. She has won a Guggenheim fellowship, and her work is included in the permanent collections of the Metropolitan Museum of Art and the High Museum of Art.

Donald Furst

Furst is a professor in the Department of Art and Theatre at the University of North Carolina at Wilmington. His work has appeared in exhibitions organized by the Mint Museum of Art, Charlotte; the Chicago Center for the Print; and the Leicester City Gallery, England; and is featured at the Fogg Art Museum of Harvard University; the Nelson-Atkins Museum of Art, Kansas City; and the Oregon Art Institute, Portland.

Maud Gatewood

Gatewood is a native of Caswell County, North Carolina, and now resides in Chapel Hill, North Carolina. A former Fulbright scholar and university faculty member, Gatewood has shown her work in solo and group exhibitions across the United States. She is a recipient of the North Carolina Governor's Award in Fine Arts and the painting award from the American Academy of Arts and Letters and the National Institute of Arts and Letters.

Jonathan Green

Green is originally from Gardens Corner, South Carolina. In 1996, University of South Carolina Press published *Gullah Images*, a collection of his works reflecting his native region. Green has had four solo national traveling exhibitions and 37 solo exhibitions in museums and cultural centers since 1982. He received an Honorary Doctorate of Fine Arts from the University of South Carolina.

Phil Moody

Born and educated in Scotland, Moody is Associate Professor of Art at Winthrop University in Rock Hill, South Carolina. His awards include the 1998 Carnegie Foundation South Carolina Professor of the Year, a South Carolina Arts Commission Artist's Project Grant, and several Rock Hill Arts Council Project Grants.

Tom Stanley

Stanley is director of the University Galleries at Winthrop University in Rock Hill, South Carolina. His recent projects include co-curating "Still Worth Keeping: Communities, Preservation, and Self-Taught Artists" for the South Carolina State Museum and "Gene Merritt Drawings" for the Collection de l'Art Brut in Lausanne, Switzerland.

Gerald Steinmeyer

Steinmeyer is a resident of Stokesdale, North Carolina. A 1968 graduate of the North Carolina School of the Arts, he is a Fogel Scholarship recipient. In 1982, he completed fresco studies in Florence and Venice, Italy. His work is displayed at the Kennedy Center for the Performing Arts and in a number of corporate and private collections.

Holly Taylor

Taylor is a native of Rocky Mount, North Carolina, and a graduate of the University of North Carolina at Chapel Hill. She is exploring a career in the culinary arts and is an amateur photographer.

Roger Winstead

Born and raised in Rocky Mount, North Carolina, Winstead is Director of Photography at NC State University and now lives in Raleigh. A photojournalist at *The News & Observer* for 10 years, Winstead has literally photographed the state of North Carolina from Manteo to Murphy.

Sources: Data and Analysis

Buchanan, Walter M. *Economic and Social Conditions of Negroes as Tenants and Farm Laborers in South Carolina*, Unpublished Master's Thesis. (Columbus, OH: The Ohio State University, 1929).

Cash, W.J. *The Mind of the South* (New York: Alfred A. Knopf, Inc., 1941).

Chernow, Ron. *Titan: The Life of John D. Rockefeller, Sr.* (New York: Random House, 1998).

Children's Defense Fund, *Children in the States: 1998 Data*, <http://www.childrensdefensefund.org/states/data.html>

Duke Endowment, The. *Annual Report of the Hospital Section*, 1926.

Durden, Robert F. *Lasting Legacy to the Carolinas: The Duke Endowment, 1924-1994* (Durham, NC: Duke University Press, 1998).

——— *The Dukes of Durham: 1865-1929* (Durham, NC: Duke University Press, 1987).

Ervin, Sam J., Jr. *Preserving the Constitution: The Autobiography of Senator Sam J. Ervin, Jr.* (Charlottesville, VA: The Michie Company, 1984).

Grantham, Dewey W. *The South in Modern America: A Region at Odds* (New York: HarperCollins, 1994).

Hemmingway, Theodore. *Beneath the Yoke of Bondage: A History of Black Folks in South Carolina, 1900-1940* (Ann Arbor, MI: University Microfilms International, 1987).

Herbers, John. *The New Heartland: America's Flight Beyond the Suburbs and How It Is Changing Our Future* (New York: TimesBooks, 1986).

Hobbs, Samuel H. *North Carolina: Economic and Social* (Chapel Hill, NC: University of North Carolina Press, 1930).

——— *North Carolina: An Economic and Social Profile* (Chapel Hill, NC: University of North Carolina Press, 1958).

Hovey, Harold A., and Kendra Hovey. *CQ's State Fact Finder* (Washington, DC: Congressional Quarterly, 1998).

Key, V.O. *Southern Politics in State and Nation* (Vintage, 1949).

Kids Count Data Online, <http://www.aecf.org/kidscount/index.htm>

Lefler, H.T., and A.R. Newsome. *North Carolina* (Chapel Hill, NC: University of North Carolina Press, 1954).

MDC, Inc. *The State of the South* (Chapel Hill, NC: MDC, 1996).

——— *The State of the South 1998* (Chapel Hill, NC: MDC, 1998).

Measuring Our Progress, A Report to the North Carolina Progress Board (1997).

Measuring Up to the Challenge: A Prosperous North Carolina in a Competitive World, A Report of the Commission for a Competitive North Carolina (1995).

National Institute for Literacy, *The State of Literacy in America: Estimates at the Local, State, and National Levels* (1998).

North Carolina Office of Minority Health, *North Carolina Minority Health Facts* (Raleigh, NC: State Center for Health Statistics, July 1998).

The Official Web Site of North Carolina, <http://www.state.nc.us>

Odum, Howard W. *Southern Regions of the United States* (Chapel Hill, NC: University of North Carolina Press, 1937).

Peirce, Neal R. *The Border South States* (New York: W.W. Norton & Company, 1975).

Peirce, Neal R., and Jerry Hagstrom. *The Book of America: Inside 50 States Today* (New York: W.W. Norton & Company, 1983).

Postsecondary Education Opportunity, The Mortenson Research Seminar on Public Policy Analysis of Opportunity for Postsecondary Education (March and May, 1998).

… "Rubella Breaks out in Robeson." (Raleigh, NC: *The News & Observer*, August 1, 1998).

Schulman, Bruce J. *From Cotton Belt to Sunbelt* (Durham, NC: Duke University Press, 1994)

State of South Carolina Public Information Homepage, <http://www.state.sc.us>

Tindall, George B. *The Emergence of the New South, 1913-1945* (Baton Rouge: Louisiana State University Press, 1967).

United States Bureau of the Census. *Census of Population*, various years 1910-1990. (Washington, DC).

——— *Historical Statistics of the United States, Colonial Times to 1970* (Washington, DC).

——— *Statistical Abstract of the United States*, various years 1919-1998. (Washington, DC).

——— *Religious Bodies, 1926* (Washington, DC).

——— *State and Metropolitan Area Data Book Web Site*, <http://www.census.gov/statab/www/smadb.html>

United States Bureau of the Census Web Site, <http://www.census.gov>

United States Bureau of Economic Analysis. *Survey of Current Business*, various years 1921-1998. (Washington, DC).

Williams, G. Croft. *Social Problems of South Carolina* (Columbia, SC: The State Co., 1928).

Winter, William F. "Race: An Intractable Issue" (New Orleans, LA: Speech to the Council on Foundations conference, *The Roles and Responsibilities of Foundations on the Issue of Race*, April 20, 1999).

Wolfe, Thomas. "The Men of Old Catawba" from *From Death to Morning*. (New York: Scribner's, 1935).

Sources: Literature and Art

Editor's Note Regarding *Hog Series CCXX: The Duke Endowment/In Memory of George Autry*.

George Autry took great joy in gathering art for this volume. He worked with Maud Gatewood, his "old buddy," in selecting art for the dust jacket. And he spent much time conversing with Tarleton Blackwell, whose *Hog Series* consists of more than 200 pieces with multiple images of the South and its history. As a result of their conversations, Blackwell created *Hog Series CCXX*, partly representing the increasing diversity of the South's population. He finished the work on the weekend when George died, and he named it in George's honor.

Editor's Note Regarding *The Miracle of the Loaves and Fishes*.

Shay Lombardo served as associate artist of the mural; John Scales and Gerald Steinmeyer served as muratores; Liz Clayton, Sterling Nicholson, and Erica Nicholson served as assistant artists. Steinmeyer designed the tabernacle frame, which peaks at 17 feet, as an integral part of the composition. Germanton (NC) United Methodist Church is open for the public to view the fresco from 8:00 a.m. to 6:00 p.m. Monday through Saturday and 1:00 p.m. to 6:00 p.m. on Sundays.

Applewhite, James. *History of the River* (Baton Rouge: Louisiana State University Press, 1993).

Chappell, Fred. (Baton Rouge: Louisiana State University Press, 1985).

Chitwood, Michael. *The Weave Room* (Chicago: University of Chicago Press, 1998).

Conroy, Pat. *The Water is Wide* (New York: Bantam Books, 1987).

Down and Out in the Great Depression: Letters from the Forgotten Man, ed. R.S. McElvaince. (Chapel Hill, NC: University of North Carolina Press, 1983).

Gatewood, Maud. *re-visions* (Greensboro, NC: Weatherspoon Art Gallery, University of North Carolina at Greensboro, 1994).

Green, Jonathan. *Gullah Images* (Columbia, SC: University of South Carolina Press, 1996).

Humphreys, Josephine. *Dreams of Sleep* (New York: Viking, 1984).

New Stories from The South: 1998, The Year's Best, ed. Shannon Ravnel. (Chapel Hill, NC: Algonquin Press, 1998).

Price, Reynolds. *A Whole New Life* (New York: Plume, 1982).

Proctor, Samuel D., and W.D. Watley. *Sermons from the Black Pulpit* (Valley Forge, PA: Judson Press, 1984).

The Rough Road Home: Stories by North Carolina Writers, ed. Robert Gingher. (Chapel Hill, NC: University of North Carolina Press, 1992).

Spielman, David G., and William W. Starr. *Southern Writers* (Columbia, SC: University of South Carolina Press, 1997).